IMAGES
of America

KENTUCKY'S
FAMOUS
RACEHORSES

KEENELAND RACE COURSE. This photograph of a horse race at the Keeneland Race Course was taken by C. Morgan-Cornett, an equine photographer and horsewoman. (Photograph by and courtesy of C. Morgan-Cornett.)

IMAGES
of America

KENTUCKY'S
FAMOUS
RACEHORSES

Patricia L. Thompson

ARCADIA
PUBLISHING

Published by Arcadia Publishing
Charleston SC, Chicago IL, Portsmouth NH, San Francisco CA

Printed in the United States of America

Library of Congress Control Number: 2009934775

For all general information contact Arcadia Publishing at:
Telephone 843-853-2070
Fax 843-853-0044
E-mail sales@arcadiapublishing.com
For customer service and orders:
Toll-Free 1-888-313-2665

Visit us on the Internet at www.arcadiapublishing.com

To Eugene Donnelly Thompson
March 30, 1939–March 17, 2009.

This book is dedicated to Gene Thompson, who lived
most of his life in Lexington, Kentucky.
He left behind his wife, three children, five grandchildren, and
numerous friends who will remember his life and his wonderful spirit.
Gene was a quiet, gentle man who preferred animals to most people.
He was very selective in choosing his friends and was
most content spending time with his family.
Gene was a good man and an excellent horseman!

CONTENTS

ACKNOWLEDGMENTS

I want to thank Neville Collins and Gene Thompson for their stories and advice; Linda Alicea of Middlebrook Farm and Tony Battaglia of Claiborne Farm for their stories and willingness to work with me on this endeavor; and Tony Battaglia and others at Claiborne Farm for their stories. Thanks to Jimmy Williams at Keeneland Race Course for granting me permission to photograph Keeneland; Helen Alexander, owner of Middlebrook Farm, for allowing me to photograph horses on her farm; Edward Stephens, manager of Elmendorf Farm, for his pictures and the history of Elmendorf; the people at Old Friends Dream Chase Farm for their time and stories about their horses; Karen Pulliam for the evenings and occasional weekends she helped me with formatting pictures; and many others who shared their stories. A special thanks to equine photographer James Archambeault for his graciousness in allowing me to use his work and the valuable time and advice he shared and C. Morgan-Cornett of Versailles, Kentucky, for her photo contributions and her knowledge of horses. I must thank Ann Hayes and Anne Peters of Three Chimneys Farm for their valuable assistance and photographs and the people at the Lexington History Museum—without their knowledge and assistance I couldn't have gotten a lot of the information I am sharing with you. I thank the people of the Keeneland Library, the Kentucky Horse Park, and the wonderful people all over this country and Canada who provided me with stories, photographs, and lots of good wishes. Thank you to Heather Watson; without her assistance, this book would not have made it to publication. I thank my children—Mark Thompson, Stacey Sindelar, and Matthew Thompson; I taught them to do their best and finish what they started. They were my reason for finishing. I thank all of you.

Copyright permission was verbally granted by James Archambeault for his work.

INTRODUCTION

Most of the time, when someone talks about a racehorse, only the horse's racing or breeding statistics are discussed. This book does not cover that information. Instead, I am sharing the personality of the horses, some of the little known facts about them, and their particular quirks.

When I began researching information for this book, I mentioned to an old friend and well-respected horseman, Neville Collins, the difficulties in getting the information I wanted regarding the personality of the horse. Collins told me I needed to talk to the grooms: stallion grooms, broodmare grooms, and race track grooms. I found that frequently horsemen who are normally rather shy and not particularly talkative will easily talk about the horses—their horses.

Horses are perceptive. They can sense fear and strength, and they know affection when they get it. Some horses are practical jokers, some are mean, some have a streak of independence, some are grateful, and some are skittish. They all develop their own individual personality.

Arrange for several horse farm tours; each tour will add to your knowledge. On a tour, the guide will point out interesting things about the area before even setting foot onto the farm proper. Once on the farm, visitors are met by a farm employee who will know the farm's history and horses. The guide may go over the tour rules for visitors' protection. Racehorses can be skittish and are probably worth more money than the average tourist.

The person introducing visitors to the horses loves these animals. On a tour, visitors will discover where and how the horses live, their daily routine, and the particular quirks that will endear the horse to the visitors or cause them to use extra caution. Either way, tourists see a beautiful animal that has done his or her job well. These horses can be derby and breeders' cup winners, including some of the most famous and expensive horses in the world. The guides will bring the horse to the visitors for an up-close experience, and visitors may even be allowed to give the horse a carrot or mint. Often, tourists are allowed to take photographs. The horses are quite used to it, and some will automatically strike a pose.

While I do not speak car or electronics, I do speak a little horse. If horse is not your native tongue, please see the Glossary on page 126 to assist in your translation.

One

BREEDING IS
NOT EVERYTHING

THE CELEBRATED HORSE LEXINGTON (5 YRS. OLD) BY BOSTON OUT OF ALICE CARNEAL.
WINNER OF THE GREAT 4 MILE MATCH FOR $ 20,000 AGAINST "LECOMPTE" TIME OF 7:26.
OVER THE METAIRIE COURSE, — NEW ORLEANS, APRIL 2ND 1855.
WON IN 7:19¾ !!!

LEXINGTON, 1850–1875. A blood bay standing just over 15 hands high, Lexington's earnings totaled $56,500. He spent his final years blind, a disability that fortunately did not affect his offspring. Lexington's first appearance on a racetrack was in 1853 under the name Darley in the Association Stakes for three year olds. At that time, a horse would be entered in a race that might be 4 miles long but divided into heats. Half way through the heats, he was sold to Richard Broeck, who renamed him Lexington. He stood his first season at stud in 1855, was sold to R. A. Alexander for $15,000, and stood at stud at Woodburn Farm until his death. Lexington founded a line of offspring unequalled by any other sire in this country or England. Lexington also sired Gen. Ulysses S. Grant's favorite horse, Cincinnati. During the Civil War, horses were conscripted from Kentucky farms to serve as mounts in battles. Lexington, 15 years old and blind, was hidden to save him from this fate. His remains are currently in the Smithsonian Museum under catalogue number 16020. (Courtesy of author; artwork by L. Maurer, reprint from lith by N. Currier.)

Aristides
FIRST KENTUCKY DERBY WINNER - 1875

R. H. Polenske

ARISTIDES, 1872–1893. Aristides, owned by Hal Price McGrath, was named for McGrath's best friend, Aristides Welch, another noted horseman. Aristides won the first Kentucky Derby in 1875. He did not receive a blanket of roses because they were not given until 1896, the same year the distance of the derby was reduced to its present 1.25 miles. Aristides raced 21 times with nine wins, five places, and one show. (Courtesy of author; artwork by R.H. Polenske.)

SALVATOR, 1886–1909. Salvator was bred by Daniel Swigert of Elmendorf Farm in Lexington, Kentucky, and was born in California. Ben Ali Haggin purchased Salina, Salvator's dam, in foal. Being one of the wealthiest men in the country, he wanted the largest breeding operation in the world, so he began purchasing farms and breeding horses from everywhere that bred fine thoroughbreds. He bought Swigert's Elmendorf Farm and moved his base of operations there. Eventually Elmendorf was broken up, becoming Spendthrift, Normandy, Old Kenney, Green Gates and Clovelly Farms. Haggin had his eastern trainer chose the best young horses to take back to the East Coast. One of these horses was Salvator. (Courtesy of Anne Peters.)

SALVATOR. Salvator raced against the best of his day: Proctor Knott and Tenny. Proctor Knott was Salvator's racing nemesis as a two year old. Then along came Tenny, and the two competed for the three-year-old honors. Tenny and Salvator competed in the Suburban Handicap, and Salvator won. A match race was set up, and Salvator won that too. Salvator beat everything he ran against, so he raced the clock and beat that too. That would be his last race. Standing stud, he and Tenny were both good sires. They competed in everything, but he beat Tenny again when he died first in 1909 at age 20. (Courtesy of Anne Peters.)

SALVATOR INDUCTED. Salvator was one of the first horses to be inducted into the newly formed National Museum of Racing and Hall of Fame in 1955. (Courtesy of Anne Peters.)

BEN BRUSH 1896

BEN BRUSH, 1893–1918. Ben Brush was the first horse to win the Kentucky Derby at its modern distance of 1.25 miles. It was the 22nd running of the derby and the first to present a blanket of roses. The roses were said to be pink and white. Ben Brush was named after the superintendent of the old Gravesend Race Track to show appreciation to him for allowing the owner, African American Ed Brown, stall space when it was scarce. Ben Brush could be very tough, but when it came to his namesake, he was lenient. When others complained of his favoritism, legend says he would reply, "Not a damn one of you fellows ever named a horse Ben Brush!" People of the eastern tracks referred to Ben Brush as "an overrated little goat." Ben Brush was sold to Mike Dwyer, who had raced Ben Brush's sire, named Bramble. Ben Brush was ridden by Willie Simms, an African American considered one of the greatest riders of the day and the only African American jockey to have won the derby, the Preakness Stakes, and the Belmont Stakes. (Courtesy of author.)

SIR BARTON, 1916–1937. Sir Barton was entered in the Kentucky Derby to be the rabbit for his stable mate, Billy Kelly. A rabbit is a speed horse that sets the pace to wear the field down. Sir Barton did not know he was the rabbit and led the field from start to finish, winning the race by five lengths. Four days later, he won the Preakness Stakes and then the Belmont Stakes, where he set the American record for 1.375 miles, the Belmont Stakes distance at that time. He did all of this in just 32 days, unheard of in that day and time. In 1919, Sir Barton received America's highest honor for a racehorse—Horse of the Year. Sir Barton's most memorable race was a match race with the famous Man O' War at Kenilworth Park in Canada. The hard-track surface was too painful on his hooves, and Man O' War beat him by seven lengths. He was retired to stud in Virginia and was later sold to a rancher in Wyoming, where he died of colic. (Courtesy of author.)

Fairplay, 1905–1929. This statue of Fairplay was originally on Elmendorf Farm but currently stands at Normandy Farm, on the parcel of land they purchased from Elmendorf Farm. An extremely ill-tempered horse, he was an excellent track horse and the sire of Man O' War. (Courtesy of Elmendorf Farm.)

Omaha 1932- 1959

Omaha with jockey Wayne D Wright Aqueduct 1935

OMAHA IN HIS LATER YEARS 1950's

Omaha Kentucky Derby William Saunders jockey

Bred & owned by: Belair Stud
Trained by Sunny Jim Fitzsimmons
Ridden by William Saunders
& Wayne D Wright
Triple Crown Winner 1935
Also won, Dwyer S., Arlington Classic;
Victor Wild S. (GB), Queen's Plate (GB);
Stood initially at Claiborne Farm, KY,
then in New York
Finally in Nebraska, where he died in 1959
His remains were buried at the now-defunct
Ak-Sar-Ben racetrack
Only Triple Crown winner sired by another
Triple Crown winner (Gallant Fox).

OMAHA (USA) ch. H, 1932 22 Starts, 9 Wins, 7 Places, 2 Shows **Career Earnings: $154,755**

Sire: GALLANT FOX (USA) b. 1927				
SIR GALLAHAD (FR) b. 1920	TEDDY (FR) b. 1913	AJAX (FR) b. 1901	FLYING FOX (GB) b. 1896	
			AMIE (FR) ch. 1893	
		RONDEAU (GB) b. 1900	BAY RONALD (GB) b. 1893	
			DOREMI (GB) ch. 1894	
	PLUCKY LIEGE (GB) b. 1912	SPEARMINT (GB) b. 1903	CARBINE (NZ) b. 1885	
			MAID OF THE MINT (GB) b. 1897	
		CONCERTINA (GB) b. 1896	ST SIMON (GB) br. 1881	
			COMIC SONG (GB) b. 1884	
MARGUERITE (USA) ch. 1920	CELT (USA) ch. 1905	COMMANDO (USA) b. 1898	DOMINO (USA) blk/br. 189	
			EMMA C. (USA) b. 1892	
		MAID OF ERIN (USA) ch. 1895	AMPHION (GB) ch. 1886	
			MAVOURNEEN (GB) ch. 1888	
	FAIRY RAY (GB) ch. 1911	RADIUM (GB) b. 1903	BEND OR (GB) ch. 1877	
			TAIA (GB) b. 1892	
		SERAPH (GB) ch. 1906	ST FRUSQUIN (GB) br. 1893	
			ST. MARINA (GB) ch. 1895	
Dam: FLAMBINO (USA) b. 1924				
WRACK (GB) b. 1909	ROBERT LE DIABLE (FR) b. 1899	AYRSHIRE (GB) br. 1885	HAMPTON (GB) b. 1872	
			ATALANTA (GB) b. 1878	
		ROSE BAY (GB) b. 1891	MELTON (GB) b. 1882	
			ROSE OF LANCASTER (GB) ch. 1878	
	SAMPHIRE (GB) b. 1902	ISINGLASS (GB) br. 1890	ISONOMY (GB) b. 1875	
			DEAD LOCK (GB) ch. 1878	
		CHELANDRY (GB) b. 1894	GOLDFINCH (GB) ch. 1889	
			ILLUMINATA (GB) br. 1877	
FLAMBETTE (FR) b. 1918	DURBAR (FR) b. 1911	RABELAIS (GB) b. 1900	ST SIMON (GB) br. 1881	
			SATIRICAL (GB) ch. 1891	
		ARMENIA (USA) ch. 1901	MEDDLER (GB) b. 1890	
			URANIA (USA) ch. 1892	
	LA FLAMBEE (FR) b. 1912	AJAX (FR) b. 1901	FLYING FOX (GB) b. 1896	
			AMIE (FR) ch. 1893	
		MEDEAH (FR) ch. 1905	MASQUE (FR) b. 1894	
			LYGIE (FR) ch. 1900	

Became the only Triple Crown winner to sire a Triple Crown winner was bred and owned by the Belair Stud. 17 Starts 11 - 3 - 2, $328,165. Also sired Granville. Flares Ascot Gold Cup winner 1938. Belmont Stakes winner 1936. Died November 13, 1954. Buried at Claiborne Farm.

FLAMBINO (USA) b. 1924 Owner Belair Stud. Breeder William Woodward. Winnings 9 Starts 4 - 1 - 2, $9,575. At 3 - Won Gazelle S. 3rd Belmont S. Coaching Club American Oaks. also dam of Ascot Gold Cup winner Flares, & stakes winner Fleam. Flambette's racraced daughter La France became the dam of Jacola and Johnstown. Another daughter, Gillette, produced the champion racemare Gallorette and her sister Gallita.

...on his way to England where he won the Queens Plate in 1936

OMAHA, 1932–1959. He was the 1935 Triple Crown Winner. His stallion performance was rather unremarkable, and he was pensioned to a farm south of Omaha, Nebraska. After being pensioned, he would frequently be taken to the race track as a promotional stunt, and it is said that when the gate bell rang to begin a race, he would lope down the track inside the rail. The fans loved it—and him. When he died, he was buried in the Circle of Champions at the Ak-Sar-Ben track (Nebraska spelled backwards). The University of Nebraska–Omaha obtained the racetrack land when it closed. Omaha's burial spot was lost during building construction. Where he actually is today remains a mystery. Tales of Omaha say the grave is supposedly next to a home economics and culinary arts classroom building. When the recipe of the day flops, the unfortunate student is told to "Give it to Omaha," meaning throw it out the window. On their way to a test, supposedly students nod toward Omaha's grave for luck. (Courtesy of author.)

"Bull Lea" the Sire of many famous Race Horses

Bull Lea, 1935–1964. This dark brown horse from Calumet Farms had an unassuming appearance and a tendency to be crotchety. He did not like his nose touched, and he definitely wanted to be fed on time. He ran the 1938 Kentucky Derby but finished a poor eighth. Bull Lea's name was made in his progeny with sons like Citation, the 1948 Triple Crown winner, and Hill Gail, the 1952 Kentucky Derby winner. Another son, Iron Liege, won the 1957 Kentucky Derby because jockey Bill Shoemaker, on Gallant Man, misjudged the finish line. On that foggy day, Shoemaker stood up too early in his stirrups, slowing down Gallant Man, and Bill Hartack rode Iron Liege on by for the win. (Courtesy of author.)

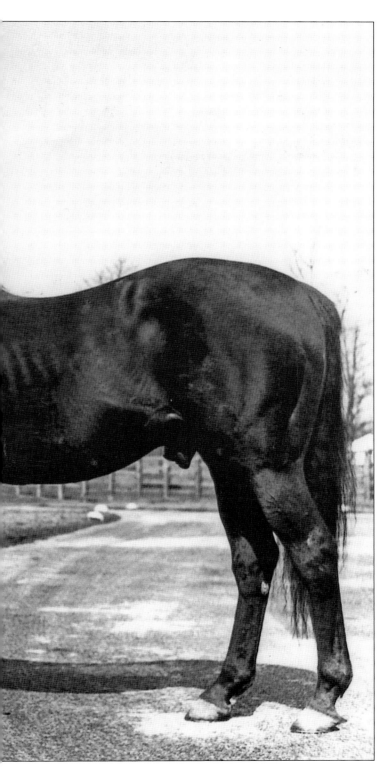

MAN O' WAR, 1917–1947.
Man O' War was bred by
Maj. August Belmont II
and was named by Eleanor
Belmont in honor of her
husband's participation in
World War I. Man O' War
was sold by Major Belmont,
who felt that the war
would prevent his racing
that year's yearling crop.
He sold Man O' War for
only $5,000 at the Saratoga
sales in 1918. In August
1919, Man O' War ran
against Whitney Stable's
horse, Upset, in Saratoga's
Sanford Memorial Stakes.
Regaining lost ground
from a bad start, his rider,
Johnny Loftus, made a
judgment error, going to
the inside and boxing in
Man O' War. Ironically,
his only career loss was
to the colt Upset. Stable
employees claimed
that Man O' War had
nightmares for weeks after
his only defeat. Apparently
first he got mad and
then he got even. He
beat Upset by a length in
the Grand Union Hotel
Stakes. And he never
lost again. Many people
think Man O' War won
the Kentucky Derby and
the Triple Crown, but he
never raced in Kentucky;
therefore, he could not
and did not win the derby
or the Triple Crown.
(Courtesy of author.)

MAN-O-WAR
Clarence Kummer
up

MAN O' WAR. Like most horses, Man O' War had his quirks. He came from a line of unmanageable horses. His grandsire, Hastings, was supposedly famous for biting other horses during races. While he refrained from biting other horses, he had a puzzling habit of chewing on his hooves. Man O' War, nicknamed "Big Red," was retired to stud at Faraway Farm in Lexington, Kentucky. He was as successful a sire as he was a racehorse. Big Red sired champions such as Crusader, American Flag, Clyde Van Duson, Bateau, and the most famous of all—1937 Triple Crown winner War Admiral. When a number of his offspring in the U.S. Cavalry were killed in World War II, Man O' War was given the military rank of major. His stud groom, Will Harbut, told many tales about Big Red's racing days. Many say the bond between Man O' War and Harbut was so strong that Man O' War actually died of a broken heart only days after Harbut's death. Man O' War died on November 1, 1947, after suffering a heart attack. He was given a military funeral with full honors. More than 2,000 people attended the funeral, which included nine eulogies and a bugler playing "Taps," which was broadcast by radio across the country. His story lives on and is a treat for die-hard fans. He was the first horse to be embalmed and is now buried at the Kentucky Horse Park in Lexington, Kentucky. His race record is 21 starts, 20 wins, and one second. Harbut's infamous words, "He wuz da mostest hoss," will live forever. (Courtesy of Kentucky Horse Park.)

Ipset, W. Knapp up, beating Man O'War, J. Loftus, up
olden Broom, F. Ambrose, up "The Sanford" Saratoga, 1919

C.C.Cook

UPSET, 1919–1920. Rumor had it that when Upset (far right) beat the famous Man O' War (center), it coined a major sports term. Supposedly, not long after Upset beat Man O' War, the term "upset" became a part of sports language to describe an unexpected defeat. Whether this is true or not, it makes a good sports story, and Upset was one appropriately named horse. C. V. Whitney, the owner of Upset, was so thrilled with the win over Man O' War that he shared his fortune with everyone in the barn. The farrier that shoed Upset was the great-grandfather of the future governor of New York, David Paterson. Whitney gave him a house in Fort Greene in Brooklyn. It became the home where Governor Paterson himself later lived. (Courtesy of author; photograph by C. C. Cook.)

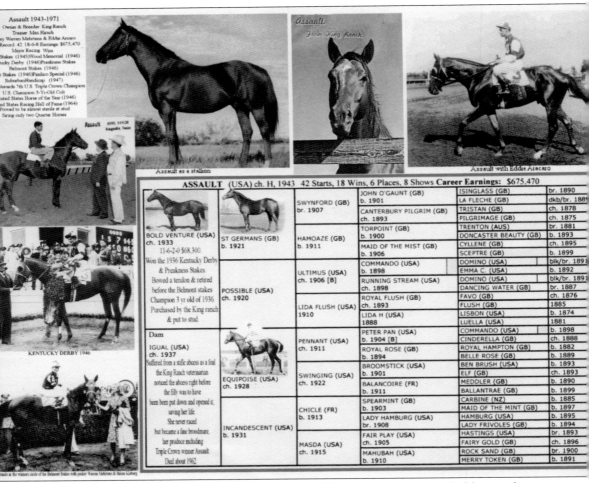

Assault 1943–1971
Owner & Breeder King Ranch
Trainer Max Hirsch
Jockey Warren Mehrtens & Eddie Arcaro
Record 42 18-6-8 Earnings $675,470
Major Racing Wins
...Stakes (1945) Wood Memorial (1946)
...tucky Derby (1946) Preakness Stakes
... Belmont Stakes (1946)
... Stakes (1946) Pimlico Special (1946)
...Suburban Handicap (1947)
...Awards 7th U.S. Triple Crown Champion
U.S. Champion 3-Yr-Old Colt
...United States Horse of the Year (1946)
...ted States Racing Hall of Fame (1964)
...Proved to be almost sterile at stud
...Siring only two Quarter Horses

Assault as a stallion

Assault From King Ranch

Assault with Eddie Arcaro

KENTUCKY DERBY 1946

ASSAULT (USA) ch. H, 1943 42 Starts, 18 Wins, 6 Places, 8 Shows Career Earnings: $675,470

				br. 1890
BOLD VENTURE (USA) ch. 1933	ST GERMANS (GB) b. 1921	SWYNFORD (GB) br. 1907	JOHN O'GAUNT (GB) b. 1901 — ISINGLASS (GB) / LA FLECHE (GB)	ISINGLASS (GB) br. 1890 / LA FLECHE (GB) dkb/br. 1889
			CANTERBURY PILGRIM (GB) ch. 1893	TRISTAN (GB) ch. 1878 / PILGRIMAGE (GB) ch. 1875
		HAMOAZE (GB) b. 1911	TORPOINT (GB) b. 1900	TRENTON (AUS) br. 1881 / DONCASTER BEAUTY (GB) b. 1893
			MAID OF THE MIST (GB) b. 1906	CYLLENE (GB) ch. 1895 / SCEPTRE (GB) b. 1899
	POSSIBLE (USA) ch. 1920	ULTIMUS (USA) ch. 1906 [B]	COMMANDO (USA) b. 1898	DOMINO (USA) blk/br. 1891 / EMMA C. (USA) b. 1892
			RUNNING STREAM (USA) ch. 1898	DOMINO (USA) blk/br. 1891 / DANCING WATER (GB) br. 1887
		LIDA FLUSH (USA) 1910	ROYAL FLUSH (GB) ch. 1893	FAVO (GB) ch. 1876 / FLUSH (GB) 1885
			LIDA H (USA) 1888	LISBON (USA) b. 1874 / LUELLA (USA) 1881
Dam IGUAL (USA) ch. 1937	EQUIPOISE (USA) ch. 1928	PENNANT (USA) ch. 1911	PETER PAN (USA) b. 1904 [B]	COMMANDO (USA) b. 1898 / CINDERELLA (GB) ch. 1888
			ROYAL ROSE (GB) b. 1894	ROYAL HAMPTON (GB) b. 1882 / BELLE ROSE (GB) b. 1889
		SWINGING (USA) ch. 1922	BROOMSTICK (USA) b. 1901	BEN BRUSH (USA) b. 1893 / ELF (GB) ch. 1893
			BALANCOIRE (FR) b. 1911	MEDDLER (GB) b. 1890 / BALLANTRAE (GB) b. 1899
	INCANDESCENT (USA) b. 1931	CHICLE (FR) b. 1913	SPEARMINT (GB) b. 1903	CARBINE (NZ) b. 1885 / MAID OF THE MINT (GB) b. 1897
			LADY HAMBURG (USA) br. 1908	HAMBURG (USA) b. 1895 / LADY FRIVOLES (GB) b. 1894
		MASDA (USA) ch. 1915	FAIR PLAY (USA) ch. 1905	HASTINGS (USA) br. 1893 / FAIRY GOLD (GB) ch. 1896
			MAHUBAH (USA) b. 1910	ROCK SAND (GB) br. 1900 / MERRY TOKEN (GB) b. 1891

BOLD VENTURE (USA) ch. 1933
11-6-2-0 $68,300
Won the 1936 Kentucky Derby & Preakness Stakes
Bowed a tendon & retired before the Belmont stakes
Champion 3 yr old of 1936
Purchased by the King ranch & put to stud

Dam
IGUAL (USA) ch. 1937
Suffered from a stifle abcess as a foal the King Ranch veterinarian noticed the abcess right before the filly was to have been put down and opened it, saving her life. She never raced but became a fine broodmare, her produce including Triple Crown winner Assault. Died about 1962

ASSAULT, A.K.A "CLUB-FOOTED COMET," 1933–1971. Assault was a crippled horse who many thought would never race. He was nearly destroyed as a weanling after stepping on a sharp object—thought to be a surveyor's stake—with his right front foot. But this tough son of Bold Venture proved what heart could do. He won the 1946 Triple Crown. (Courtesy of author.)

ASSAULT. The following winter, Assault matured into a handsome horse with a demanding personality and a huge sense of humor. He was always hungry, and if his grooms did not feed him, he would charge them. He also found great fun dumping his exercise riders. If the exercise rider was not paying enough attention, Assault would suddenly jump to the side, leaving his rider on the ground as he went galloping around the track. Born a Texan, Assault died a Texan in 1971. He is buried at the King Ranch in Kingsville, Texas. (Both courtesy of author.)

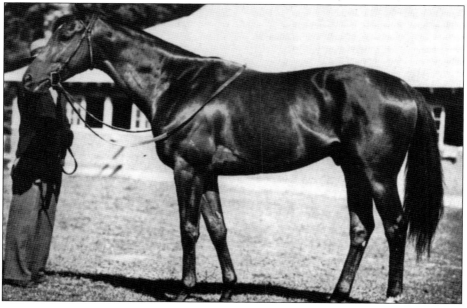

SEABISCUIT, 1933–1947. His grandsire was Man O' War. His dam was Swing On, but he was named after his sire, Hardtack, who was named for a type of cracker eaten by sailors, known as a sea biscuit or hardtack. Seabiscuit was a small, homely, knobby-kneed horse who had a tendency to be lazy and loved to sleep. He would sleep 10 hours a day if his trainer let him, and running was not a particular interest for him. Trainer Tom Smith understood the horse. He used unorthodox training methods, including hiring feisty jockey Red Pollard, to bring Seabiscuit around. Seabiscuit and Red understood each other. He finally began winning. His most famous race was against Triple Crown winner War Admiral, sired by Man O' War. The two famous racehorses met in the race of the century on November 1, 1938. Seabiscuit took the lead right from the start. He allowed War Admiral a brief moment of leading by a nose, only to then look War Admiral in the eye and use his usual late burst of speed to win the race by four lengths. This race earned him the 1938 Horse of the Year title. Seabiscuit suffered a ruptured suspensory ligament in his front left leg. Most horses were retired after suffering this serious injury. Seabiscuit recuperated at Ridgewood Ranch along with Red, who had suffered a crushed leg. Everyone assumed the careers of both were over, but they helped each other and miraculously raced together again. Seabiscuit is buried at Ridgewood Ranch in California at an undisclosed location. (Courtesy of author.)

WAR ADMIRAL, 1934–1959. The best and most memorable of Man O' War's offspring, War Admiral was a striking dark brown colt out of dam Brushup. He was foaled in 1934 at Faraway Farm in Lexington, Kentucky. War Admiral held up the Belmont Stakes race for several minutes, pulling starters through the gate, and then was finally allowed to start on the outside. He stumbled badly, regrouped, and went on to win the last leg of the coveted Triple Crown in 1937, earning him the title Horse of the Year. War Admiral was a great racehorse, but another horse on the West Coast was also doing well. This West Coast horse was not as pretty, but he certainly inherited his grand sire's affinity for running and winning. The country demanded a match race. Seabiscuit, grandson of Man O' War, would run against War Admiral, son of Man O' War. Both horses had similar running styles, and they were of similar stature. And neither liked to lose. On November 1, 1938, War Admiral and Seabiscuit met at Pimlico Race Course in a winner-take-all race for a $15,000 purse. Because of War Admiral's distaste of the starting gate, the two would race with a dropped flag for a distance of 1.1875 miles. Both carried 120 pounds, and the track was fast. War Admiral took an early lead, but the final four lengths belonged to Seabiscuit. This match race was to be the legacy of both horses. War Admiral retired to stud with a record of 21 wins in 26 starts. He was a successful stallion, leading the sire list 11 times, and was the top broodmare sire twice, producing 40 stakes winners. War Admiral died in 1959 and was buried at the base of his father's statue at the Kentucky Horse Park in Lexington, KY. (Courtesy of author.)

WHIRLAWAY
Eddie Arcaro
up

WHIRLAWAY, 1938–1953. Foaled on Calumet Farm, Whirlaway's fans dubbed him "Mr. Long Tail" because of his extremely long tail. Trainer Ben Jones referred to him as "The Half Wit" and "Knucklehead" because of his erratic running. He would run down the middle and then veer out to the outside rail. Once he even banged into it and still won the race. Whirlaway liked things his way. If a jockey tried to veer him in another direction, the horse was inclined to throw a tantrum. He preferred routine. His racetrack independence cost him some races, but he won most of the important ones, including the Kentucky Derby, the Preakness Stakes, and the Belmont Stakes in 1941, making him a Triple Crown winner. Whirlaway ruptured nerve tissue and died in France in 1953. His body was returned to Calumet Farm and remains there today. He was inducted into the Hall of Fame in 1959. (Courtesy of author.)

CITATION, 1945–1970. The 1948 Triple Crown winner, Citation, was born at Calumet Farm in Lexington, Kentucky. Warren Wright, the owner of Calumet Farm, thought an overseas mare was the way to get a winner, so he simply purchased Hydroplane II. World War II was his biggest problem, as he had to get his newly purchased mare to the United States. The Atlantic Ocean was heavily dotted with enemy ships, so his safest route was the long way, via the Pacific Ocean. Citation won eight of his nine starts as a two year old. He made such an impressive three-year-old debut that it was surmised he was destined to become a horse to be remembered. All thoroughbred horses celebrate January 1 as their official birthday in regards to racing. This colt was born in April, so he was running against more experienced horses. He was the first million-dollar winner, with a total of $1,085,760. Citation died in 1970 at age 25. He spent his career being compared to Man O' War, a comparison that is still debated. (Both courtesy of author.)

CITATION
1945:
CITATION IS BORN ON
APRIL 11 IN
LEXINGTON, KENTUCKY.

CRÈME DE LA CRÈME, 1963–1977. Crème de la Crème made his history as a result of a devastating, life-threatening injury. He began his racing career in 1965 with only two starts, and he won both. By 1966, after only 11 starts, his career earnings were $164,240. Crème de la Crème was then syndicated. Shares were sold for $40,000 each. His fateful day in racing was in the running of the Quaker City Handicap on October 12, 1966. He shattered his right knee. This type of injury normally would be the end of a horse's life, but Dr. Jacques Jenny at the New Bolton Center led a team that saved his life with a groundbreaking surgical technique. Months after the surgery, he was allowed to stand stud at the Spendthrift Horse Farm in Lexington, Kentucky. In 1977, he was humanely euthanized after an unknown illness. (Courtesy of Gene Thompson.)

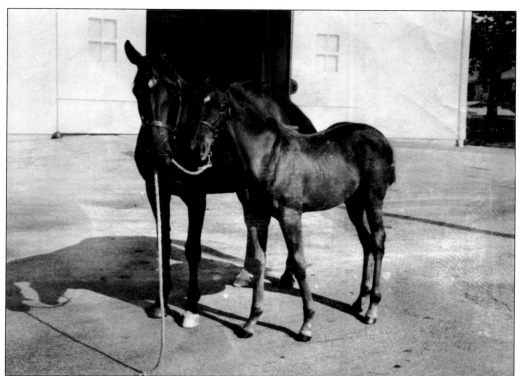

BALDERDASH. A broodmare at Bwamazon Farm in Winchester, Kentucky, Balderdash was a special horse to Gene Thompson. The picture was taken and sent to Thompson with this note on the back. (Courtesy of Gene Thompson.)

014

My dearest Gene,

I just thought you might enjoy looking at my first born. I just hope your first one is as nice.

The men around here are so kind as you can see they let me lead my baby when ever we go out.

Thank you for taking such great care of me at the track only song I wasn't a CICADA, I am sure that I will become another MISTY MORN.

Your first true Love,
"Balderdash"

29

FORWARD PASS

From a painting by Charles Carroll
The collection of Mrs. Julian Fortney

FORWARD PASS, 1965–1980. Forward Pass's biggest claim to fame was the controversial 1968 Kentucky Derby when, after finishing second, he was declared the winner. He was definitely a graded stakes winning horse, but in 1968, he ran second to Dancer's Image. Dancer's Image was disqualified after urinalysis indicated that "bute" was found. Phenylbutazone, or bute, was legal at many tracks but not at Churchill Downs. The drug is a pain medication frequently given to horses with non-serious injuries to allow them to continue to work comfortably. Since 1968's controversial decision, research has proven that phenylbutazone does not enhance the horse's ability to run; therefore, Churchill Downs no longer considers it an illegal substance. (Courtesy of author.)

DANCER'S IMAGE

From a painting by Charles Carroll
The collection of Mrs. Julian Fortney

DANCER'S IMAGE, 1965–1992. Dancer's Image was a proven graded stakes winner. At three years of age, he headed to Kentucky for the first leg of the coveted Triple Crown races. He had a history of sore ankles. Dr. Alex Harthill, known as "Derby Doc," was hired to treat the horse and gave him a commonly used pain killer called phenylbutazone. If treated with this drug six days before the Kentucky Derby, it should have been out of Dancer's Image's system. However, phenylbutazone showed up in a urinalysis that was performed after the race. Dancer's Image was disqualified and denied the win. He died in Japan at age 27, where he had been standing stud. Dancer's Image was the first and last horse ever to be disqualified in the Derby as of this time. (Courtesy of author.)

FANFRELUCHE, 1967–1999. Fanfreluche was a champion. She won many prestigious races and earned numerous awards and honors, including the Eclipse Award and the Sovereign Award for Canadian Horse of the Year. In June 1977, while she was in foal to Secretariat, Fanfreluche was kidnapped from Claiborne Farm in Bourbon County, Kentucky. It was suspected to be an inside job. Apparently the kidnappers panicked and turned her loose on a country road near Tompkinsville, Kentucky, nearly 190 miles from her home. She was found by a family, who took her in at their farm. Almost six months later, she was identified by the tattoo inside her upper lip and returned to Claiborne Farm. She gave birth to a colt named Sain Et Sauf, which means "safe and sound" in English. Fanfreluche died of old age and is buried at the former Big Sink Farm, now Three Chimneys, in Woodford County. Donna Lee Barnette of Blue Spruce Farm in Richmond, Kentucky, had a real love for Fanfreluche. Her personal letters suggest she may have purchased or assisted with the purchase of a headstone for Fanfreluche's grave. Barnette used to put flowers on Fanfreluche's grave and had requested that flowers continue to be put on the grave after her death. The photograph of Fanfreluche with foal is with her last foal, Red Alydar. (Both courtesy of Anne Hayes, Three Chimneys Farm.)

SECRETARIAT, 1970–1989. Secretariat is one of the most famous horses. People thought of him as another Man O' War or Citation. He made his racing debut at Aqueduct on the Fourth of July in 1972. He did not win that day. But 11 days later, at the same track, Secretariat showed what he was made of by coming from behind and winning by four lengths. He was on the road to Kentucky, and everyone knew it. With a loss behind him, he came to the 1973 Kentucky Derby to show what he could do. Secretariat not only won his chance at immortality that day, but also did so in record-breaking time. His next stop would be in Maryland for the Preakness Stakes, and once more he performed magnificently, winning again in record-breaking time. The next leg of the infamous Triple Crown was the New York Belmont Stakes. It is a race that many a horse cannot handle because of the distance. But it was his crowning glory. Secretariat won the 1.5-mile race by 31 lengths and in record-breaking time. Nicknamed "Big Red" like Man O' War, Secretariat retired from racing to stand stud at Kentucky's famous Claiborne Farm. Secretariat died on October 4, 1989. (Above, courtesy of author; below, photograph by and courtesy of author.)

RUFFIAN, 1972–1975. This big filly is still considered to be one of the greatest of all time. Ruffian won the Filly Triple Crown in 1975. Her trainer gave her high praise when he compared her with Secretariat and suggested she might be even better. Her final race was at Belmont Park in July 1975 in a match race with Foolish Pleasure. The same jockey had ridden both horses and chose to ride Ruffian that day. Counting both television and track spectators, it is estimated nearly 19 million people watched the race. Ruffian had a bad start, hitting her shoulder on the starting gate. Obviously in pain, she quickly took the lead and held it until the sesamoid bones in her right front leg snapped. Her jockey tried to rein her in, but she continued running. Like many before her, she hated being behind and hated to lose. Her injuries were indescribable. She was tended to immediately and underwent emergency surgery. Unfortunately, when she was coming out of the anesthesia she thrashed about so much that she injured herself more and had to be euthanized. *Sports Illustrated* considered her the only nonhuman on its list of the century's 100 Greatest Female Athletes. Ruffian was ranked 53rd. (Courtesy of author.)

SEATTLE SLEW, 1974–2002. Seattle Slew was foaled at the White Horse Acres Farm near Lexington, Kentucky. His birth was not particularly notable, and neither was his breeding. He was sold by Fasig-Tipton for a mere $17,500. He began his training in Maryland. The first and only undefeated Triple Crown winner, Seattle Slew seemed to be smart, a trait not attributed to most horses. He seemed to really like racing and had this little dance he did on the way to the post. While Seattle Slew was a highly spirited horse, he seemed to know when children were around and expressed a gentleness not normally seen in stallions. He loved having his picture taken and would willingly pose for a camera. Seattle Slew loved cold weather and snow and seemed to associate it with breeding season. He would longingly look out his stall for the arriving mares. He sired more than 100 stakes winners and a champion broodmare sire. Seattle Slew has an impressive progeny with horses like A. P. Indy (a leading sire today), Swale, and Vindication, just to name a few. (Courtesy of author; photograph by James Archambeault .)

ALYDAR, 1975–1990. Born on the famous Calumet Farm in Lexington, Kentucky, Alydar was one of the more exceptional racehorses. Alydar ran 26 times with 14 wins, 9 places, and 1 show. He raced against Affirmed 10 times, winning three of those races. Alydar was overshadowed by Affirmed, as he ran a close second to Affirmed in all three races of the Triple Crown, yet in all three races, the combined total distance was less than two lengths between the two horses. Alydar retired from racing and stood stud at Calumet in Lexington. He was an excellent sire and produced the famous Alysheba (a Kentucky Derby, Preakness Stakes, and Breeders' Club Classic winner), Strike the Gold, Althea, Alydaress, Cat Thief, and many more. In November 1990, Alydar shattered his right hind leg. Emergency surgery was performed, but the leg broke again, and he was euthanized. This happened at a time when the great Calumet was in serious financial difficulties. Alydar's death created suspicion because he was insured for $36.5 million. (Courtesy of James Archambeault.)

AFFIRMED, 1975–2001. The last winner of the coveted Triple Crown races in 1978, Affirmed (No. 6) was born at Harbor View Farm in Florida. He had an interesting racing career. He continually faced another two-year-old colt named Alydar, and they seemed to be the competition in all of their races. It got to be such a racing distraction that his trainer did not want to continually be facing Alydar, so he moved out West to prepare for the Triple Crown. The two horses did meet again at Churchill Downs—and Affirmed took it all. His earnings totaled more than $2 million. Ironically, he once again met up with his racing nemesis, Alydar, when he retired to stud at Calumet Farm. In 2001, he contracted laminitis, a fatal hoof disease, and was put down. He received the highest honor a horse can receive in death: he was buried whole wearing his original owner's colors. Typically, most horses have only their head, heart, and four hooves buried to represent wind, heart, and speed. He has been inducted into the National Museum of Racing and Hall of Fame. (Both courtesy of author; below, photograph by James Archambeault.)

JOHN HENRY, 1975–2007. John Henry was named after the folk hero John Henry, the steel-driving man. As a youngster, the equine John Henry had a habit of tearing the steel water and feed buckets off stall walls and stomping them flat. John Henry was gelded both for his orneriness as well as his lack of breeding. His sire, Ole Bob Bowers, once sold for just $900 and was not much in demand by breeders. His dam, Once Double, was an undistinguished runner and producer but was sired by Double Jay, a brilliantly fast graded stakes race winner who had proven to be a useful broodmare sire. John Henry is buried at the Kentucky Horse Park. (Courtesy of Karen Pulliam; photograph by James Archambeault.)

SPECTACULAR BID, 1976–2003.
Nicknamed "The Bid," he (No. 5) was the 1979 Kentucky Derby and Preakness Stakes winner. It was the Belmont Stakes, the third leg of the Triple Crown, that proved to be too much for Spectacular Bid. He joined many a great racehorse as a non-winner in the Belmont Stakes. His trainer reported a safety pin injury the night before the Belmont Stakes and it has been suggested that this attributed to his loss. There were other rumors about his trainer blaming the jockey, Ron Franklin. Still other stories say the trainer gave Franklin credit for a good ride and that Spectacular Bid just was not a 1.5-mile horse. Regardless of why he did not win the Belmont Stakes, he was a great horse. He was purchased for $37,000. With total earnings of almost $3 million, he earned his keep. (Above, courtesy of author; left, courtesy of Karen Pulliam, photograph by James Archambeault.)

TOO CHIC, B. 1980. Emory Alexander Hamilton purchased Too Chic, a yearling in 1980, at a dispersal sale at the King Ranch for $100,000. She was a graded stakes winner. As a three year old, she had eight starts and four wins. With great bloodlines, she later proved to be a great broodmare too. (Courtesy of Gene Thompson.)

AQUEDUCT, NEW YORK PURSE $17,000 MAY 6, 1982
EMORY G. ALEXANDER OWNER   TOO CHIC   RUBEN HERNANDEZ UP
J.W. MALONEY TRAINER   7 FUR. TIME 1:23:1
CLASSIC AMBITION 2nd   MISS LITTLE 3rd

FORTUNATE PROSPECT, B. 1981. There are rare occasions when a racehorse has a respectable track record and an even better stallion record. Fortunate Prospect is one of those horses. Fortunate Prospect, by Northern Prospect and out of Fortunate Bid, had 39 starts and 13 wins. He has a better-than-average progeny line to his record. He has sired 28 stakes winners, and his total progeny earnings to date are more than $30 million. He was not Kentucky-bred, but he now lives at Old Friends in Georgetown, Kentucky, after the farm where he stood stud was liquidated. (Courtesy of author.)

ALTHEA
Aykroyd,Alexander & Groves,Owners D.Wayne Lukas,Trainer
1Mile 1:34.4 Laffit Pincay,Up   Juliet's Pride 2nd
Gumboy 3rd 9-14-83   Thirty-sixth Running of the
DEL MAR FUTURITY (Grade 11)   DEL MAR RACE TRACK
      $150,000 Added-Estimated Gross $225,000

ALTHEA, 1981–1995. By Alydar, Althea is a great stakes winning mare. She won four races in five starts, including California's most important two-year-old races, the Hollywood Juvenile and the Del Mar Futurity. She beat colts in both races. Althea ran in the 1984 Kentucky Derby but finished a poor 19th. She is buried at Middlebrook Farm in Lexington, Kentucky. (Both courtesy of Gene Thompson.)

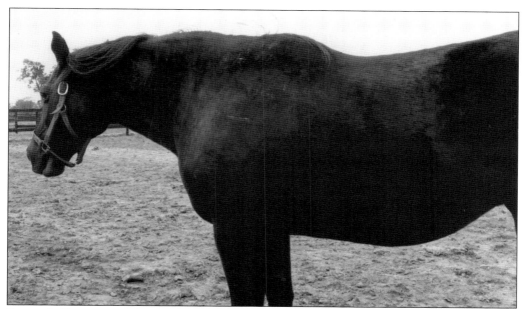

BONNIE'S POKER, B. 1982. By Poker and out of Surprise by Wise Margin, Bonnie's Poker was not particularly successful on the racetrack. She had 63 starts and only 11 wins to her name. As frequently happens to fillies and mares, she earned her recognition as a broodmare. After a complicated delivery of a colt in her later years, the courts got involved in making the decision whether to continue to breed her or allow her to be pensioned. A wise judge made the decision she should be pensioned. She resides now at Old Friends, a retirement/rescue farm in Georgetown, Kentucky. (Courtesy of author.)

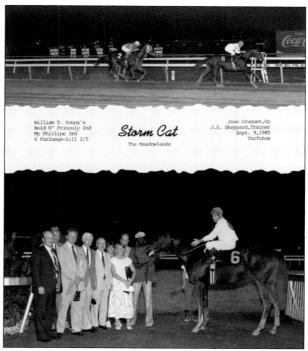

STORM CAT, B. 1983. Storm Cat was extremely well bred, but he raced only eight times, with four wins and three places. His total earnings were $570,610. He retired to stud as a three year old. He is best known for the horses he sired. Storm Cat's progeny have produced more than $117 million in earnings. His value as a sire earned him 24-hour, guarded protection. During his peak stud seasons, he commanded a fee of $500,000 for a live foal—one of the highest stud fees in the world. Storm Cat was pensioned in 2008 at age 25 and is living out his years at Overbrook Farm in Lexington, KY. (Courtesy of Gene Thompson.)

OGYGIAN, B. 1983. By Damascus and out of Gonfalon, Ogygian proved himself to be a graded stakes winner, but he suffered an ankle injury while racing and never fully recovered from it. Before being pensioned, he stood stud at Claiborne Farm in Paris, Kentucky, and in Japan. He suffered the loss of an eye in the breeding shed but that did not stop him from producing numerous stakes winners and 11 graded stakes winners. When acquired by Old Friends in Georgetown, Kentucky, from Japan, he arrived wearing a lucky amulet. It was violet, the holy color of Buddhism. It had been given to him some time before to bring him safely home. It was his lucky charm. (Courtesy of author.)

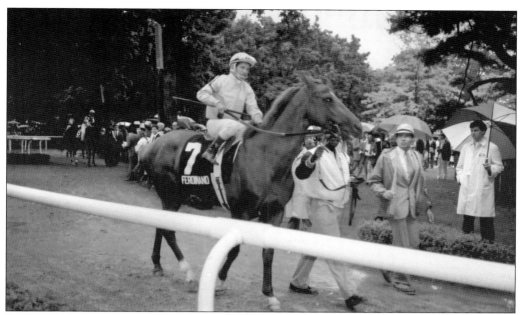

FERDINAND, 1983–2002. Ferdinand was truly an excellent racehorse, winning the 1986 Kentucky Derby, the Breeders' Cup Classic, and the 1987 Eclipse Award for Horse of the Year. However, he was most famous for being sent to the slaughterhouse in Japan. Unfortunately, Ferdinand was unsuccessful as a sire. This is perhaps the reason for the manner of his death. His name was still quite fresh in the minds of Americans and horse-racing enthusiast when his death was reported. It created such an outrage that a bill to protect racehorses from such a death was introduced to the U.S. House of Representatives (H.R. 503). The American Horse Slaughter Prevention Act passed in 2007 to ban the slaughter of horses in the United States. Also, in 2006, the New York Owners and Breeders' Association initiated the small, voluntary per-race charge called the "Ferdinand Fee" to support the Thoroughbred Charities of America and Bluegrass Charities. Now some owners include buy-back clauses in their stallion contracts to prevent this atrocity from ever happening again. (Courtesy of author.)

FUTURAL, B. 1996. Sired by Future Storm and out of Twigazuri, Futural earned $816,107 during his racing career. He resides at Old Friends in Georgetown, Kentucky. A true gentleman, he enjoys attention, polite conversation, and a good banana. (Courtesy of author.)

ALYSHEBA. He was foaled in 1984 on Hamburg Farm in Lexington, Kentucky and later sold for a mere $500,000. As a two year old, he was not particularly impressive, and as a three year old, he also was not looking great. He had a problem with knocking other horses out of his way. Being a late developer, he improved dramatically as a four year old. His lifetime earnings were $6,679,242. In the Kentucky Derby, he and jockey Chris McCarron were nearly knocked to the ground at the top of the stretch by Bet Twice, who would become a major rival. Alysheba recovered and won the 1987 derby. He then came back with another win in the Preakness Stakes. In the Belmont Stakes, Alysheba was required to race without the diuretic Lasix, which was prohibited in New York racing. He finished fourth. He was named the 1988 Horse of the Year. When pensioned, he returned to live out his years at the Kentucky Horse Park. He died in 2009 from a degenerative spinal condition. He was euthanized after he fell in his stall and was unable to get to his feet again. He is buried at the Kentucky Horse Park's Hall of Champions. (Courtesy of author.)

ALYSHEBA, 1984–2009. Alysheba is shown being welcomed by fans at the Kentucky Horse Park upon his return to Kentucky. (Courtesy of Karen Pulliam.)

SEEKING THE GOLD, B. 1985. This 23-year-old stallion made his mark in racing and as a stallion. Seeking the Gold had 15 starts with eight wins and six second places for total earnings of $2,307,000. A strong-willed horse with a tendency to bite, he once pulled off the salt block that was bolted down on the barn wall. That move caught the attention of the stallion barn grooms. They give him a wide berth and have acknowledged that he is the "boss" of that barn. They say he is not a horse to turn your back on. He quietly seeks an opportunity to grab somebody or something. Seeking the Gold was pensioned in 2008 and remains at Claiborne Farm in Paris, Kentucky. (Courtesy of Karen Pulliam.)

WINNING COLORS, 1985–2008. Winning Colors was the first of four Kentucky Derby winners for trainer D. Wayne Lucas. A filly winning against the boys is always a rush for derby goers. It takes a great horse to run like that. She would break fast and take the lead. She set the pace on that first Saturday in May 1988. She held the lead the whole way, winning by a dark-grey neck. What a race for any horse, but a filly? She did it her way. She raced as a four year old, but her campaign was riddled with breathing problems, and she was retired for breeding. The last filly to win the Kentucky Derby, Winning Colors was put down at age 23 after a bout of colic. She is buried at Greentree Farm, a division of Gainsway Farm in Lexington, Kentucky. (Courtesy of author.)

SUNSHINE FOREVER, B. 1985. Sired by Roberto and out of Outward Sunshine, Sunshine Forever earned more than $2 million in his racing career. He won the 1988 Eclipse Award for Outstanding Turf Horse. He retired from racing in 1990 and stood stud at Japan's Nitta Farm, the same farm where Ferdinand had stood. In 2004, he was pensioned to Old Friends in Georgetown, Kentucky. (Courtesy of author.)

CREATOR, B. 1986. Creator, sired by Mill Reef and out of Chalon by Habitat, was bred and owned by Sheik Mohammed bin Rashid Al Maktoum, the ruler of Dubai. Creator had a very successful racing career and stood stud at Nitta Farm with Sunshine Forever. They returned to the United States to live out their years in Kentucky. (Courtesy of author.)

SUNDAY SILENCE, 1986–2002. Sunday Silence was born at Stone Farm and was owned by A. B. Hancock III. As a weanling, he caught a virus that nearly took his life. Later he narrowly escaped death after a horse van accident. Sunday Silence beat all the odds. As a two year old, he showed his stuff, winning a maiden race by 10 lengths. He began prepping for the Kentucky Derby but still did not catch the eyes of derby goers. On a muddy track that first Saturday in May 1989, Sunday Silence took home the roses. He won the Preakness Stakes by a nose. Sunday Silence also took the Breeders Cup Classic, earning him the title of Horse of the Year and a season record of $4,578,454. He retired to stud in 1989 and was sold to Yoshida's Shadai Farm in Japan. In Japan, he proved himself a worthy stallion, producing foals that would go on to earn millions. Sunday Silence died in August 2002. He is buried at Shadai Farm in Japan. (Courtesy of author.)

UNBRIDLED, 1987–2001. This 1990 Kentucky Derby winner placed second in the Preakness Stakes and was not in the money in the Belmont Stakes. He was named the Eclipse Award winner as a three year old. During the derby, it was reported that trainer Carl Nafzger gave the horse's elderly owner, Frances Genter, the stretch call because of her poor vision, "He's going to win! He's going to win! Oh, Mrs. Genter, I love you!" Unbridled raced through 1991 before retiring with a career record of eight wins, six places, and six shows in 24 starts and $4,489,475 in earnings. He sired nine crops of winners. He died unexpectedly at age 14. (Courtesy of author.)

LEAVE SEATTLE, B. 1988. Leave Seattle, by Seattle Slew and out of Leave Me Alone, had only three starts and no wins. It is unknown why his racing ability was lacking. He has good bloodlines, and he had a respectable career standing stud. He escaped going to a slaughter auction and spent time at a boarding stable prior to arriving at a safe haven for horses. He has a sweet disposition and will live out his remaining years enjoying his retirement at Old Friends in Georgetown, Kentucky, one of the few rescue farms that will take stallions. (Courtesy of author.)

KIRI'S CLOWN, B. 1989. Kiri's Clown is by Foolish Pleasure and out of Kris. He was not a horse who liked to work or train—he liked to race. Kiri's Clown was a grade stakes winner who earned more than $1 million in his racing career. He is currently pensioned at Old Friends in Georgetown, Kentucky. (Courtesy of author.)

AWAD, B. 1990. Awad was sired by Caveat and out of Dancer's Candy. He was a Grade I stakes winner and earned $3,270.131 on the track. These days he enjoys entertaining guest at Old Friends in Georgetown, Kentucky, and rolling carrots in his mouth. (Courtesy of author.)

BULL IN THE HEATHER, B. 1990. It is appropriate that this horse by Ferdinand and out of Heather Road lives out his retirement years at Old Friends. The slaughter of his famous sire, Ferdinand, was part of the inspiration for the development of Old Friends. Bull in the Heather was not the racehorse his father was, but he gave it a good try, earning a tad more than $500,000. (Courtesy of author.)

WALLENDA, B. 1990. Sired by Gulch and out of So Glad, Wallenda was named after a high-wire act known as the Flying Wallendas. Not the usual way to earn winnings, Wallenda won a five-horse photo finish in the 1993 Louisiana Derby. He earned more than $1 million in his racing career. He now lives at Old Friends. (Photographs by and courtesy of author.)

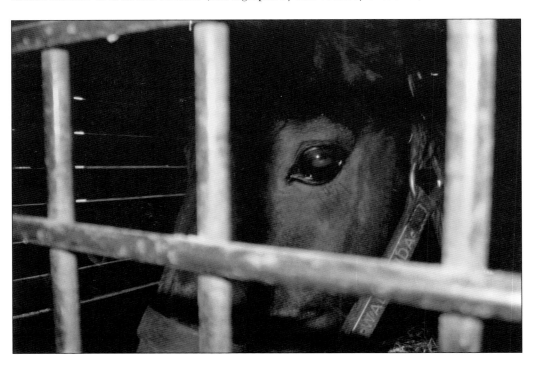

Sea Hero, b. 1990. Trained by seasoned trainer Mack Miller and owned by Paul Mellon, Sea Hero was the result of a lifetime of breeding and praying. He won the 1993 Kentucky Derby, ridden by jockey Jerry Bailey. It was not a charted race; Bailey said he took the race as it was given to him. The derby was only Sea Hero's second victory on a dirt track in four career wins, and the horse rewarded his backers with $27.80, $12.80, and $8. He won six of 24 starts for lifetime earnings at nearly $3 million. Sea Hero was retired to stud in 1993, producing numerous stakes winners. (Courtesy of author.)

WILLIAMSTOWN, B. 1990. By Seattle Slew and out of Winter Sparkle, Williamstown is a graded stakes winner with $360,884 total earnings. He sired 22 winners but was declared infertile in 2007. There were plans to euthanize him when Aubrey Insurance contacted Old Friends, and the rest is history. Visit Williamstown now at Old Friends. (Courtesy of author.)

YES IT'S TRUE, B. 1996. By Is It True and out of Clever Monique, this gave him the name Yes It's True. It definitely must be true because his progeny have earned more than $19 million. Yes It's True had 22 starts and total earnings of $1,080,700. He stands at Three Chimneys Farm in Kentucky. His stud fee is $22,500. (Courtesy of C. Morgan-Cornett.)

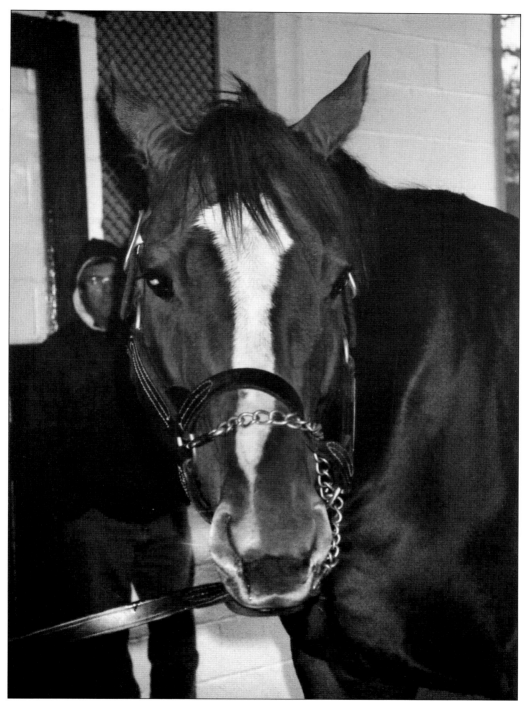

EDDINGTON, B. 2001. Eddington had 17 starts and made the board all 17 times. He retired because of an injury at age three, with total earnings of $1,216,270. He now stands stud at Claiborne Horse Farm in Paris, Kentucky. He covers about 120 mares per year, and his stud fee is $7,500 per cover, standing and nursing. (Courtesy of Karen Pulliam.)

GO FOR GIN , B. 1991. Trained by Nick Zito, Go For Gin started in 19 races, won five, and was in the money 14 times. His most famous race was the 1994 Kentucky Derby. It was a sloppy track. Chris McCarron was up, and Go for Gin won that day. He seemed, from previous races, to prefer a muddy track. He was definitely a graded stakes horse, placing in both the Preakness Stakes and Belmont Stakes following his derby win. Go for Gin retired from racing to stud in 1995 at Claiborne Farm in Paris, Kentucky. He has since been sold and moved out of state. He sired Albert the Great, who had lifetime earnings of more than $3 million. His offspring have made him a money horse. (Courtesy of author.)

STRIKE THE GOLD, B. 1988. This 1991 Kentucky Derby winner, bred by Calumet Farm and sold to BCC Farm, is the oldest living derby winner after Alysheba died in 2009. Strike the Gold also won the Bluegrass Stakes in 1991 and the Nassau County Handicap and the Pimlico Special in 1992. His racing earnings were $3,457,026. At age five, he was retired to stud at Ben Walden's Vinery near Midway, Kentucky. He did not prove to be a successful breeder in the United States; however, he was sold to the Jockey Club of Turkey and bred to the daughter of Shareef Dancer. They produced the 2001 colt Soberly, who earned $5.5 million. (Courtesy of author.)

THUNDER GULCH, B. 1992. This 1995 Kentucky Derby winner took D. Wayne Lucas on a surprise trip to the winner's circle. Thunder Gulch was a third-string horse who paid racegoers $51 for the win that day. He also won the Belmont Stakes that year. Injuring a leg, Thunder Gulch retired from racing. He stands at Coolmore/Ashford Stud and is a shuttle stallion, traveling to Chile, Argentina, and Australia. His best offspring so far is Point Given, who won the Preakness Stakes and Belmont Stakes in 2001. Stallions have a tendency to be mean and high strung, but according to Thunder Gulch's handlers, he is "very gentle in nature and just a nice horse to be around." (Courtesy of author.)

SILVER CHARM, B. 1994. Silver Charm, the 1997 Kentucky Derby and Preakness Stakes winner, lost the Belmont Stakes to a horse named Touch of Gold. On that Saturday, the higher-priced metal won. (Courtesy of author; photograph by John Archambeault.)

KONA GOLD, B. 1994. Kona Gold, by Java Gold and out of Double Sunrise, retired from racing with earnings of $2,293,284 and a record of 14-7-2. He is a good-tempered horse with a feisty attitude. He can be visited at the Kentucky Horse Park. (Both courtesy of author.)

WILL'S WAY, B. 1993. The son of Easy Goer and dam Willamae, this Grade I stakes winner started 13 times with six wins and lifetime earnings of $954,400. His progeny have earned more than $5 million. Will's Way was pensioned to Old Friends. He has a sweet disposition and enjoys the daily visitors. (Courtesy of author.)

PULPIT, B. 1995. By A. P. Indy and out of Preach, Pulpit is an exceptional breeding stallion with the bloodlines of Seattle Slew, Mr. Prospector, and Secretariat. Pulpit has produced 657 foals. With bloodlines like this, it is no wonder his progeny have earned more than $38 million, making him a successful stallion. He only started six times but had four wins and one second for total racing earnings of $728,200. His fee as a stallion in 2010 is $60,000, standing and nursing. (Courtesy of author.)

REAL QUIET, B. 1995. Real Quiet (No. 8) is a slim-framed horse with knobby knees. While not as famous as much of his competition, he took his time and proved himself to be more horse than anyone imagined by becoming a Grade I stakes horse. He won the 1998 Kentucky Derby and was closer to winning the Triple Crown than any other horse since Affirmed in 1978. Real Quiet won the derby and the Preakness Stakes, but he lost the Belmont Stakes by a nose. Not bad for "The Fish," as his trainer, Bob Baffert, called him for his thin face. Real Quiet currently stands stud at Three Chimneys Farm in Midway, Kentucky. (Courtesy of author.)

War Emblem, b. 1999. War Emblem won the 2002 Kentucky Derby and the Preakness Stakes. He stumbled running the Belmont Stakes, lost ground, and while making a valiant effort, he tired and lost the race. War Emblem retired to stud in 2002 and was purchased by Shadai Stallion Station in Japan. The foals he has produced have proven to be quality runners, but War Emblem is just not interested in breeding to a mare. It has been suggested that his immaturity is to blame for his lack of interest in mares. He was separated from other stallions in the hopes that he would not be so intimidated and would have an opportunity to sexually mature with confidence. It has even been suggested that bringing in another stallion may assist with War Emblem's interest in the breeding process. This prompts many to wonder, "Is War Emblem gay?" (Courtesy of author.)

CHARISMATIC, B. 1996. He is best known as the closest challenger for the Triple Crown since Affirmed in 1978. As a third-generation descendant of Secretariat via Weekend Surprise, he is a blood relation to A. P. Indy. A 31-1 long shot in the 1999 Kentucky Derby, he won but still had not earned the respect he was due. In the Belmont Stakes, he was favored at 2-1 odds but faded and lost. His jockey, Chris Antley, jumped off Charismatic and help up his left front leg. It was later found the horse had broken his leg in two places. Antley's action possibly saved Charismatic's life. The horse underwent surgery, but the injury ended his racing career. He currently stands at stud at Iburi Stallion Station in Japan. The moment of Chris Antley jumping off and holding up Charismatic's broken leg was chosen by racing fans as the 1999 National Thoroughbred Racing Association Moment of the Year. (Courtesy of Karen Pulliam; photograph by James Archambeault.)

KUDOS, B. 1997. This graded stakes winner had 24 starts and only seven wins but earned $1,238,000 on the racetrack. Primarily a West Coast racetrack horse, he was bred in Kentucky by Jerry and Ann Moss. He now resides at Old Friends. (Courtesy of author.)

ATELIER, B. 1997. Atelier was a Breeders' Cup starter for owner Helen Alexander of Middlebrook Farm in Lexington, Kentucky, running fourth in the 2001 Distaff. Atelier won nine races in her career, topped by a stakes win, the 2002 Molly Pitcher at Monmouth Park in New Jersey. Out of her 22 starts, she had a 9-4-1 record and earned $741,114. She is a gentle mare by nature, and she resides as a broodmare at Middlebrook Farm in Lexington. Gene Thompson would whistle, and she would come up to him. Atelier understood he genuinely cared about her and would not let anything happen to her. (Courtesy of author.)

CIGAR, B. 1990. By Palace Music and out of Solar Slew, Cigar was named for a navigation intersection for airplanes. His owner, Allen Paulson, was famous for naming his horses after aviation checkpoints. A Hall of Famer, Cigar became the first American horse to win 14 consecutive races, only to be surpassed by Citation and Buckpasser. Cigar was a slow starter in his racing career. He did not break his maiden until 1993. He began to give a glimmer of what he could do at age four. As a five year old, he took off, and there was no stopping him. With Jerry Bailey up, Cigar decidedly won the Breeders' Cup Classic in record time. Most horses would be retired from racing by age six. Instead Cigar went to Dubai to try racing on sand and under lights in the $4 million inaugural Dubai World Cup. He won. After numerous retirement parties, Cigar finally retired to the Kentucky Horse Park with a total earnings just shy of $10 million. (Courtesy of author.)

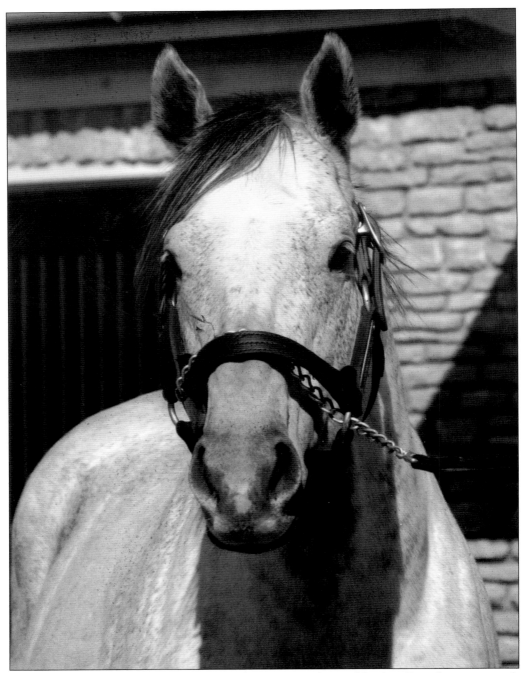

EXCHANGE RATE, B. 1997. Exchange Rate, by Danzig and out of Sterling Pound, is a gray with impressive bloodlines. He had 15 starts, winning six, placing twice, and showing two times. Exchange Rate's total earnings were $479,803. His real success has been as a sire. Exchange Rate was the top juvenile sire of 2008 and the second-leading sire of two-year-old stakes horses. He raced until age four and retired to stud at Three Chimneys Farm in Midway, Kentucky. His stud fee in 2010 is $25,000, standing and nursing. (Courtesy of C. Morgan-Cornett.)

DANTHEBLUEGRASSMAN, B. 1999. Dan was bred in Kentucky at Ledgelands Farm. The horse has so-so breeding, but he was a proven graded stakes winner, having won the Grade I and Grade II Gold Rush Stakes. He even earned a position in the 2002 Kentucky Derby but was scratched after his last-place finish in the Santa Anita Derby. Danthebluegrassman continued campaigning until age six, when he was retired. Everybody seems to love the underdog, and Dan is no exception. He was liked so well that donations were made to purchase him and bring him to live at Old Friends in Georgetown, Kentucky. When he arrived, it was noted that he had been well cared for and was a sweet horse by nature. Love the fly mask! (Courtesy of author; photograph by Beth Shannon.)

POPCORN DEELITES, B. 1998. Popcorn Deelites, by Afternoon Deelites out of Turquoise Gal, had 58 starts and 11 wins in his racing career. He raced for six years, earning nearly $60,000. He was visible in the film *Seabiscuit* (2003), breaking from the starting gate. Now pensioned, he lives at Old Friends. (Courtesy of author.)

RIVA WAY, B. 1998. This gelding is by Tinners Way and out of Yia Yia. Although he is descended from great bloodlines, he raced for only five years, mainly in claiming races. When injuries prevented him from racing, he was pensioned to Old Friends in Georgetown, Kentucky. (Courtesy of author.)

SPECIAL RING, B. 1997. Special Ring is a gelding by Nureyev and out of Ring Beaune. He began his racing career in France. A Grade I stakes winner, he raced for eight years. Special Ring was donated to Old Friends by his owner, Jack Preston. He earned more than $900,000 on the racetrack. (Courtesy of author.)

MONARCHOS, B. 1998. Monarchos is famous for having the second-fastest winning time in Kentucky Derby history. He won the 2001 race with a time of 1:59:97. The fastest time is claimed by the 1973 Triple Crown winner, Secretariat, at 1:59:40. Monarchos stands stud at the Nuckols Farm in Midway, Kentucky. (Courtesy of author.)

FUNNY CIDE, B. 2000. Funny Cide, winner of the 2003 Kentucky Derby, was named after his dam and sire, Belle's Good Cide and Distorted Humor. The first gelding to win the derby since 1929, he was gelded because of an undescended testicle. It seems Funny Cide found his situation uncomfortable when running; gelding him restored his good humor when racing. (Courtesy of author.)

SMARTY JONES, B. 2001. Owned by Chappy and Pat Chapman, Smarty Jones was named to honor Pat Chapman's late mother, Milly "Smarty" McNair. Bobby Camac was his trainer, but he and his wife, Maryann, were murdered. That and failing health caused Chappy to sell most of his horses. The Chapmans sold the farm, keeping only four horses in training, including Smarty. While training, Smarty Jones reared up and smashed his head on the top of the starting gate, fracturing his skull and falling to the ground unconscious and bleeding. The bones around his left eye were so badly broken there was talk of removing his eye, but he recuperated and began to show promise. He won the 2004 Kentucky Derby, becoming the first unbeaten Kentucky Derby winner since Seattle Slew. He stands at Three chimneys Farm in Midway, Kentucky. (Courtesy of Leah Sindelar.)

GOOD REWARD, B. 2001. Good Reward is by Storm Cat and out of Heavenly Prize, both champions. He won multiple Grade I races and favors his dam. He raced through 2006 with 26 career starts and made the board 21 times. He earned a total of $1,087,687. Good Reward stands stud at Three Chimney Farm in Midway, Kentucky, and earns $5,000, standing and nursing. He covered 200 mares his first two seasons. (Courtesy of C. Morgan-Cornett.)

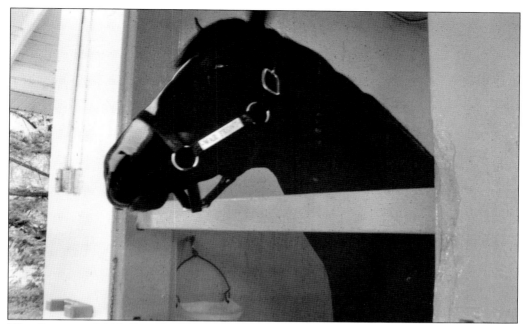

WAR FRONT, B. 2002. Born by Danzig and out of Starry Dreamer, War Front started a total of 13 times and made the board 10 of those starts. He was a Grade I winner and made the board two more times before he was retired to Claiborne Farm in Paris, Kentucky, in 2006. War Front's lifetime racing earnings are $424,205. He commands a stallion fee of $10,000 for standing and nursing. (Courtesy of author.)

FLOWER ALLEY, B. 2002. Flower Alley was born in 2002, a chestnut colt by Distorted Humor and out of Princess Olivia. His grandsire on both sides of his immediate pedigree is Mr. Prospector. Being a spring foal, he was going to be behind in size and maturity when he began racing because all thoroughbred foals celebrate their birthday on January 1, regardless of the actual birth date. Flower Alley had a total of 14 starts and earned a total of $2,533,910. (Courtesy of C. Morgan-Cornett.)

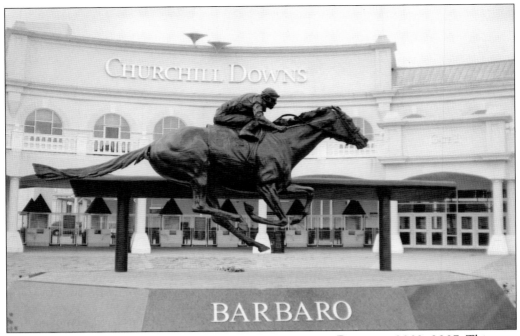

BARBARO

BARBARO, 2003–2007. This Kentucky horse won the American Class Race, but it was the 2006 Florida Derby that made Barbaro a definite contender for the 2006 Kentucky Derby. Undefeated, he went into the derby as a favorite and easily won the roses. Two weeks later, tragedy struck at the start of the Preakness Stakes when Barbaro broke a leg in three places. It was a horrific injury, and he was sent to the New Bolton Center in Pennsylvania for surgery. The public showed their love for him by sending thousands of get-well cards and flowers to him. Barbaro survived his surgery but later developed laminitis in his left hind leg. He had more surgery to remove separated tissue but was unable to recover satisfactorily. He was euthanized in January 2007. His statue stands in front of Churchill Downs as a tribute to this magnificent fallen horse. (Both courtesy of author.)

FIRST SAMAURAI, B. 2003. First Samaurai is out of Freddie Frisson and by Giant Causeway. His grandsire is Storm Cat. First Samaurai was anticipated to be a 2006 Kentucky Derby contender, but after a poor start in the Blue Grass Stakes at Keeneland and running fifth, the consensus was that he was a decent runner for about a mile, but he would not do well beyond that. His racing career is eight starts, five wins, one place, and one show. His earnings were $915,075. He entered stud in 2007, and his fee is $30,000 for standing and nursing. (Courtesy of author.)

HORSE GREELEY, B. 2004. Horse Greeley by Storm Cat and out of Chili Chatte had six starts, earning a total of $225,460. His best success is winning the Grade II Del Mar Futurity. With his good breeding, it is hoped he will produce offspring that will become grade winners. His current stud fee is $6,500 for a live foal. (Courtesy of author.)

CURLIN, B. 2004. Curlin was bred by Fares Farm in Lexington and was named for a black slave from Western Kentucky who fought in the American Civil War. He is the son of Smart Strike and out of mare Sheriff's Deputy. Curlin was co-owned by disbarred lawyer Shirley Cunningham Jr., who was convicted in the federal fen-phen fraud case. Curlin was the 2007 Horse of the Year and won the Jockey Club Gold Cup, the Breeders' Cup Classic, and the 2009 Dubai World Cup. Curlin started 15 times and earned $10 million. Curlin currently stands stud at Lane's End Farm. His current fee is $75,000 for a foal who stands and nurses. There has been some talk about breeding Curlin to Rachel Alexandra, the 2009 Horse of the Year and the first filly to win the Preakness Stakes in 85 years. (Courtesy of author; photograph by Saylor Photography.)

EIGHT BELLES, 2005–2008. Eight Belles, a lovely grey filly by Unbridled Son and out of Away, started 10 times, won five of them, and was on the board all but one race. Her total earnings are $708,650. Her lineage to Raise a Native, who had a history of leg problems, seems to have passed a similar vulnerability on to Eight Belles. On that fateful derby day in May 2008, Eight Belles ran second to Big Brown only to break both front ankles. She was humanely euthanized there on the racetrack. She will always be remembered on Kentucky Derby day. The big feature race is the Kentucky Derby; the other races that day are considered the "undercard," with the Eight Belles Stake named in her honor. (Courtesy of author; artwork by Virginia M. Bradberry.)

Big Brown, b. 2005. Big Brown was named in honor of United Parcel Service (UPS) by the company's owner, Paul Pompa Jr. Trained by the colorful Rick Dutrow and ridden by Kent Desormeaux, Big Brown easily won the first two legs of the Triple Crown. Dutrow said Big Brown winning the Belmont Stakes was "a foregone conclusion." Desormeaux pulled Big Brown up in the home stretch, saying something was wrong: "I had no horse." No abnormality was ever found. Later it was said that a photograph revealed a dislodged shoe on the right hind leg, which may have caused Big Brown's poor performance that day. Big Brown was retired to stand stud at Three Chimneys Farm in 2008 and commands a fee of $55,000 for standing and nursing. (Courtesy of author.)

Rachel Alexandra, b. 2006. Rachel Alexandra, the daughter of Medaglia d'Oro and mare Lotta Kim, was foaled in 2006 at the Stonestreet Stables in Central Kentucky. She may be the best filly in the country for 2009, if not the best horse of the year. A beautiful, 16-hand filly, she has not let anyone down. Rachel Alexandra is exceptional because she won the Kentucky Oaks by 20 lengths. She also won the second leg of the coveted Triple Crown, the Preakness Stakes, by one length, beating the Kentucky Derby winner Mine That Bird. Calvin Borel rode Mine That Bird in the Kentucky Derby, but when given the opportunity to ride Rachel Alexandra in the Preakness Stakes, he chose to ride her instead because he felt she was the better horse. She runs with her heart. She has earned her reputation as a phenomenal horse by winning the Woodward at Saratoga Spring, New York, in September 2009 and having won 10 of 13 races for a totaling earnings of $2,498,354. Azeri remains the all-time leading female with more than $4 million in earnings. (Courtesy of author.)

Mine That Bird, b. 2006. Sometimes the horse that is supposed to win does not. The 135th running of the 2009 Kentucky Derby was exactly one of those days. A 50-1 shot gelding came running from dead last to take home the roses. Mine That Bird, purchased for only $9,500, changed the lives of his Texan trainer, Chip Woolley, and his Cajun jockey, Calvin Borel. It is every American's dream to make it, and this day it happened for Woolley and Borel. Mine That Bird arrived at Churchill Downs in a horse trailer pulled by a pickup truck. Woolley was on crutches with a broken leg. He came to Kentucky an unknown, but he left with everyone knowing his name. This derby became a race to cheer about because the underdog won. Mine That Bird later ran second in the Preakness Stakes, beaten by filly Rachel Alexandra. It was in the Preakness Stakes that everyone realized he was not just a fluke, as originally thought. (Courtesy of author.)

FOALS PLAYING. This young foal is on an Old Frankfort Pike farm. He appears to wonder what that long hairy thing is attached to his backside. (Courtesy of C. Morgan-Cornett.)

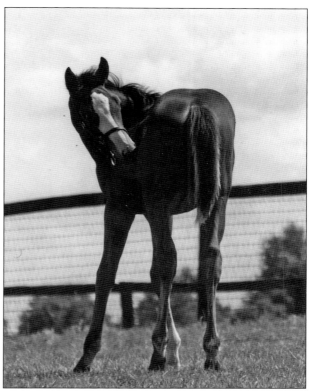

TWO MARES RELAXING. These two friends are content with each other's company on this late summer afternoon. (Courtesy of C. Morgan-Cornett.)

HORSES IN THE EARLY SPRING IN KENTUCKY. Look, dandelions! Time to be rid of the winter coats. Horses' winter coats are long and shaggy looking, but when warm weather arrives, they are groomed, and all the shedding hair comes out. (Courtesy of C. Morgan-Cornett.)

HORSES BEING WALKED BACK TO THE BARN. These horses are going back to the barn at the end of an evening playing outside. (Courtesy of C. Morgan-Cornett.)

Two

THE BACKSIDE OF RACING

BLACK BESS, MID-1800s. The Civil War Confederate general John Hunt Morgan had a favorite mare named Black Bess. (Courtesy of Anne Peters.)

BLACK BESS. In 1911, a bronze statue was unveiled in General Morgan's honor in front of the courthouse in Lexington, Kentucky. The mare was depicted as a stallion. It seems her sculptor, Pompeo Coppini, made the decision to add testicles to Bess because he felt a hero of John Hunt Morgan's magnitude should only be astride a stallion, never a mare. The unidentified author of the poem "The Ballad of Black Bess" had this to say: "So darkness comes to Bluegrass men — / Like darkness o'er them falls — / For well we know gentlemen should show / Respect for a lady's balls." With two universities in Lexington, pranks are frequently played on the statue. The Greek fraternity houses are the usual suspects behind this lady frequently displaying blue-and-white painted "jewels." (Courtesy of author.)

KEENELAND IN THE EARLY YEARS. John Oliver "Jack" Keene, owner of Keeneland Stud, had already constructed a racecourse on his farm in the 1920s. It was not unusual back then for larger farms to build their own racetracks for training purposes. Keene was also a member of a group of Bluegrass thoroughbred owners who were planning to construct a racecourse. He sold the land on Versailles Road in Lexington, Kentucky, to the Keeneland Association, and the rest is history. (Both courtesy of Harmony House Publishers; above photograph by William Strode and below photograph by Ken Weaver.)

Keeneland Race Course, Lexington, Ky.

6A-H1867

KEENELAND. Opened in 1936, Keeneland is now a National Historic Landmark. This racecourse is recognized as one of the more serene, beautiful tracks in the country. (Above, courtesy of author; below, courtesy of Harmony House Publishers, photograph by David Robertson.)

EARLY MORNING WORKOUT. Horses in training walk through the paddock area, going to the racetrack for a quick run around the track before the afternoon's races. (Courtesy of author.)

BREAKFAST. During every meet at the Keeneland racecourse, Breakfast with the Works is offered. Beginning at 7:00 a.m. on Saturday mornings, the public is invited to come out and watch the trainers work the horses. A breakfast buffet is served for a small fee. Free informational talks are given as visitors watch the same horses that may end up in the Blue Grass Stakes, the Kentucky Oaks, and the Kentucky Derby. People are encouraged to participate, take pictures, and enjoy the experience. There are activities for children, and the gift shop is open daily, even when Keeneland is not racing. As visitors are enjoying the lovely scenery and grounds, they may even catch a glimpse of someone famous! (Courtesy of author.)

CHURCHILL DOWNS, 1875. While Lexington had the first racetrack, it was approximately 100 years later that Churchill Downs opened. Racing began in the late 1700s in downtown Louisville, Kentucky. Because of the hustle and bustle associated with a growing town, racing was moved to Shippingport Island. This racecourse was called the Elm Tree Gardens. Later a new course was opened, Hope Distillery, and racing still continued on local farms in the area. Development of Churchill Downs was announced in 1874. Construction of the racetrack was funded by selling membership subscriptions. The track officially opened in May 1875 with only four races scheduled. The big race of the day was the featured race, the Kentucky Derby, pictured here. (Courtesy of author.)

CHURCHILL DOWNS. By inviting celebrities and the Kentucky Jockey Club, Churchill Downs finally showed a profit. Churchill Downs, Inc., expanded its operation and has remained the flagship of the corporation, which now encompasses racetracks and simulcast-wagering in Kentucky, Illinois, Florida, and Louisiana. It is also involved with other racing service companies. The Kentucky Derby is always the first Saturday in May. In August 2009, the derby museum suffered extensive water damage from flash flooding. Horses and humans had to move to higher ground, and all were safe. Damaged museum artifacts have been sent out for restoration. Pictured here are the famous twin spires on derby day. (Courtesy of author.)

HOPING TO WIN AND HAVE FUN. This photograph shows race day at Churchill Downs in what appears to be the 1940s. (Courtesy of author.)

OLD FRIENDS, GEORGETOWN, KENTUCKY. Old Friends is a nonprofit horse retirement farm founded and owned by Michael Blowen. Some horses have narrowly escaped the slaughterhouse. Some are full-paid pensioners. These horses are well cared for and very loved. Their only job in the world is to run, play, roll in the mud, and eat carrots and cookies. Each horse has a story. Mercer Vanderburg tells them to visitors. The horses enjoy seeing their friend with visitors and will walk up to greet everyone. They know that Mercer is going to bring them a carrot or two. There is a donation bucket in the gift shop for the "carrot fund" and all donations help support the horses. (Courtesy of author.)

NEVILLE COLLINS. Neville Collins is a quiet man. Not a big talker, he shared a moment few know about. He revealed he was the winning rider of the 1957 Plug Horse Derby, a Labor Day charity event at Red Mile Race Course in Lexington, Kentucky. The horses came from the stockyards. His horse, Friga King, was given a garland of carrots. Jockeys were paid $10 per mount. Neville has managed a few of Kentucky's famous horse farms, training and owning some quality horses. He used to exercise Nashua, a horse that had a strong tendency to throw his riders. Nashua was not just any horse; he had a record of 30 starts, 22 wins, four places, one show, and lifetime earnings of $1,288,565. Neville Collins has a gift in his knowledge of horses. (Courtesy of Neville Collins.)

LINDA ALICEA. Alicea (left), shown here with daughter Margie Keele, is a horse trainer who has done it all; she groomed, trained, and rode horses as an exercise rider. She owned and trained this horse, Bad Storm Comin (B. 1996), which she purchased as a yearling from Pope McClean's Crestwood Farm. She broke him and trained him, and he won a few nice races, including a couple of graded stakes races. Linda Alicea still works with thoroughbred horses and is a respected horsewoman. (Courtesy of Linda Alicea.)

7♣

Isaac Murphy

Won 44% of his starts, an unmatched success rate; won consecutive Derbies in 1890 and 1891

♣ 7

ISAAC MURPHY, 1861–1896. Considered one of the greatest jockeys in American history, Isaac Burns Murphy's career inspired a long list of firsts. The son of a former slave, Murphy rose to prominence in a field dominated by African American jockeys at the time. Born in Frankfort, Kentucky, he first worked as an exercise boy at Lexington stables and acquired his first race mount in 1875, at the age of 14, as a replacement rider. Murphy won that race, launching his career. He was the first rider to win three Kentucky Derbies and the only jockey to win the Kentucky Derby, the Kentucky Oaks, and the Clark Handicap in one meeting. Murphy ultimately rode 628 champions, winning 44 percent of his races. No other rider since has come close. Murphy was the first rider voted into the Jockey Hall of Fame and the first to win successive derby crowns in 1890 and 1891. This distinction went unmatched until another outstanding black rider, Jimmy Winkfield, won the coveted Run for the Roses in 1901 and 1902. Murphy was known for his skill, honesty, and loyalty. He once refused to let champion Falsetto lose the 1879 Kenner Stakes when gamblers enticed him with bribes. Murphy retired in 1892 to become a horse owner and trainer. He achieved a record 628 wins in 1,412 races during the 15 seasons he rode. Murphy died of pneumonia at age 36. He was belatedly inducted into the Jockey's Hall of Fame at Saratoga, Florida, in 1955. His body was reinterred at the Kentucky Horse Park in Lexington in 1977. This playing card featured a caricature of Isaac Murphy, while the opposite side shows the Kentucky Derby winners cup and blanket of roses. (Both courtesy of author.)

SPORT KINGS GUM

EDDIE ARCARO

EDDIE ARCARO, 1916–1997. Arcaro is a Hall of Fame jockey born in Cincinnati, Ohio. He is the only jockey to have won the Triple Crown twice. He won the Kentucky Derby five times and the Belmont Stakes six times and has the most wins in the Preakness Stakes. Arcaro won his first Triple Crown on Whirlaway in 1941. He repeated this feat again in 1948 on a Calumet Farm horse named Citation. Arcaro was inducted into the National Museum of Racing and Hall of Fame in 1958. He was a driving force in the creation of the Jockeys' Guild. He was affectionately called "Banana Nose" by the other jockeys. He also worked as a television racing commentator and as a public relations officer for a Las Vegas casino before retiring in Miami, Florida. (Both courtesy of author.)

– No. 69 –
EDDIE ARCARO
(HORSE RACING)

Born in Cincinnati, Ohio on February 19, 1916, Arcaro is considered by many to be the greatest jockey in the history of American Thoroughbred horse racing. At the age of 16, he ran his first race at the Agua Caliente racetrack in Tijuana, Mexico and built a reputation as an up-and-coming star. In 1938, he earned his first Kentucky Derby victory aboard Lawrin and he would win that race five times over the course of his storied career. Three years later, he captured the Triple Crown with victories at the Preakness Stakes and Belmont Stakes on Whirlaway. The only man to lead two horses to the Triple Crown, his second victory came in 1948 as Citation was the best in the field. A founding member of the Jockeys' Guild, the six-time United States Champion Jockey retired in 1962 after winning a remarkable 4,779 races and earning over $30,000,000 in winnings.

This card is part of Series B of noted athletes and sportsmen. The complete series will include leaders in every branch of sport. START YOUR COLLECTION NOW.

SPORTKINGS™

PAT DAY, B. 1953. Born in Brush, Colorado, Pat Day began his career in rodeos. At 4-foot-11-inches and around 100 pounds, he was encouraged to be a jockey. Day won the Eclipse Awards for Outstanding Jockey in 1984, 1986, 1987, and 1991. He received the 1985 George Woolf Award and the 1995 Mike Venezia Award. He rode in the first 21 Breeders' Cups and in 21 Kentucky Derbys. Day was inducted into the Racing Hall of Fame in 1991. He won the 1992 derby on Lil E Tee. A hip injury ended his riding career. Day retired as the leading rider at Keeneland in Lexington, Kentucky, and at Churchill Downs in Louisville, Kentucky. He is the official spokesperson for the Racetrack Chaplaincy of America and enjoys his retirement in Crestwood, Kentucky. (Courtesy of author.)

JOCKO AND THE LAWN JOCKEYS. On a freezing night in December 1776, Gen. George Washington crossed the Delaware River to launch a surprise attack against British troops. Jocko Graves, a 12-year-old African American boy, wanted to join the battle, but Washington said he was too young. Instead, Washington gave Jocko the job of looking after the horses and asked him to keep a lantern blazing along the Delaware River to mark the spot where his men should return. When Washington and his men returned to their horses—who were tethered to Jocko—they discovered the boy had frozen to death with the lantern still clenched in his fist. Washington was moved by his devotion to the revolution. He commissioned a statue of the *Faithful Groomsman* to stand in Graves's honor at his Mount Vernon estate. By the time of the American Civil War, these Jocko statues secretly pointed to safe houses of the Underground Railroad. Along the Mississippi River, ribbons were tied to a statue's arm; a green one represented safety, while a red ribbon meant danger. These original lawn jockey statues played a monumental role in the Underground Railroad that ushered so many African American slaves to freedom. Decades after the Revolutionary War, similar cast-iron statues appeared in jockey silks—perhaps to honor jockeys or in confusion because of Jocko's name. The clothing worn by the lawn jockeys resembled that worn by black riding jockeys, who have a glorious history. The first 13 winners of the Kentucky Derby were black. Contrary to some folks thinking that these statues are a racial slur, they are just the opposite: a memorial to Jocko Graves, a symbol of human freedom and a tribute to some of the greatest jockeys racing has ever known. This is a photograph of jockeys wearing the colors of the stable they are representing and holding a plaque indicating the name of the stable. (Courtesy of author.)

SERIOUS RACE PREPARATION. These men have arrived several hours early to prepare for the races. They are drinking coffee, reading the *Daily Racing Form*, and doing their own handicapping before the races begin. (Courtesy of author.)

BLUEGRASS STAKES DAY AT KEENELAND. Horses are saddled and jockeys are up as they head to the racetrack. This spring meet brings out a crowd, as this is a graded race and frequently the winners of this race have also won the Kentucky Derby. (Courtesy of author.)

THE PADDOCK AT KEENELAND. On an early Saturday morning, people come to watch the horses work out on the track. (Courtesy of author.)

Three

LIVING THE
SPORT OF KINGS

BEAUMONT FARM, LEXINGTON, KENTUCKY. Beaumont Farm, located on Harrodsburg Road, was founded by Hal Price Headley and, at one time, consisted of 4,000 acres. Now it is home to housing subdivisions, shopping malls, and businesses. The original farm home was where Sullivan College now stands. (Courtesy of author.)

CALUMET FARM, LEXINGTON, KENTUCKY. Calumet Farm, located on Versailles Road, was established by William M. Wright, founder of the Calumet Baking Powder Company. Originally based in Illinois, the Kentucky climate was more conducive for a horse farm. William Wright's son, Warren, took over the farm in 1932 and turned Calumet into a thoroughbred breeding and training station. Home to the famous Bull Lea, Calumet Farm produced eight Kentucky Derby winners and was also the leading breeder and owner of Preakness Stakes winners. Their colts Citation and Whirlaway became Triple Crown winners, and fillies Devona Dale, Real Delight, and Wistful won the Filly Triple Crown. (Courtesy of author.)

CALUMET TODAY. Calumet Farm won the coveted 1990 Eclipse Award for Outstanding Breeder. The same year, suspicion loomed over Calumet's business practices after the death of Alydar, a valuable stallion insured for $36 million. The farm filed for bankruptcy in 1991. In 2000, J. T. Lundy and the farm's chief financial officer, Gary Matthews, were convicted of fraud and bribery. In 1992, Henryk de Kwiatkowski purchased Calumet and saved it from possible liquidation by bankruptcy. (Courtesy of James Archambeault.)

CLAIBORNE FARM, PARIS, KENTUCKY. For horse people, going to Claiborne is like stepping on sacred ground. It was run by Arthur Hancock Sr. until 1947, when his son Arthur "Bull" Hancock took over. The farm's foundation sire was a horse named Wrack. Buckpasser, Swale, Nijinsky II, and Secretariat are buried there. Seth Hancock has now taken over the reins of management with a whole new crop of stallions, such as Eddington and Pulpit. Seeking the Gold was recently pensioned. Claiborne's top-notch stallions have earned them the respect as one of the top stallion farms in the world. This stallion at Claiborne Farm is sticking his tongue out . . . hopefully for a peppermint. (Courtesy of author.)

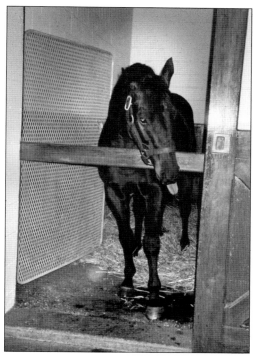

SECRETARIAT AFTER WINNING THE KENTUCKY DERBY. A movie is currently being filmed in Kentucky of Secretariat's life. It will surely showcase some beautiful scenery in bluegrass country and at Churchill Downs in Louisville, Kentucky. (Courtesy of author.)

DARBY DAN FARM, LEXINGTON, KENTUCKY. Col. E. R. Bradley originally founded this farm in 1935 from the core of Idle Hour Farm. It produced four derby winners: Behave Yourself, Bubbling Over, Burgoo King, and Brokers Tip. When Colonel Bradley died, the farm was broken up into smaller parcels and sold to different farms. Businessman John Galbreath purchased the core farm and renamed it Darby Dan. Supposedly he named it for his son, Daniel, and Darby Creek in Galloway, Ohio. Darby Dan Farm produced the 1963 and 1967 Kentucky Derby winners Chateauguay and Proud Clarion. It has now transitioned from a private farm to a commercial facility. (Both courtesy of author; below, photograph by James Archambeault.)

GREENTREE FARM, LEXINGTON, KENTUCKY. Greentree Stables, located on Paris Pike, was founded by Harry Payne Whitney. After Whitney's death, ownership transferred to his wife, Gertrude Vanderbilt Whitney. Greentree Farm became an outstanding thoroughbred nursery, producing horses such as Twenty Grand, Kentucky Derby winner Shut Out, and many others. Since 1989, Greentree has been part of the Gainesway Farm. (Courtesy of author.)

MANCHESTER FARM, LEXINGTON, KENTUCKY. This thoroughbred breeding farm, located on Rice Road, is supposedly named after the popular rendezvous point for Kentucky pioneers, Manchester Spring. Rumor has it Manchester Farm's antebellum mansion was the inspiration for the plantation home Tara in the book *Gone With the Wind*. Manchester Farm is easily recognized by the blue-and-white barns with cupolas and dormers. (Courtesy of James Archambeault.)

ELMENDORF FARM, LEXINGTON, KENTUCKY. Elmendorf is a beautiful farm that was home to a true Southern mansion known as Green Hills. It was built in 1897 by James Ben Ali Haggin for $300,000—a lot of money in those days. When Haggin died, Joseph Widener and nephew George Widener Jr. purchased a part of Elmendorf. Widener tore down Green Hills in 1929 because he did not want to pay taxes on an unoccupied house. Taxes were based on how many windows you had in your home and Green Hills had a lot of windows! The towering marble pillars are all that remain. Portions of the farm have been sold off. Normandy Farm now owns the land with the statue of Fair Play and Mahubah. Spindthrift, Clovelly, and Normandy Farms also own a portion. This farm, too, is now commercially owned by American Life Insurance. (Courtesy of author.)

ELMENDORF ENTRANCE. This is the entrance of Elmendorf Farm, which includes a self-supporting staircase. Note the intricacy of the handrail on the staircase and the hand-carved wood paneling on the walls. (Courtesy of Elmendorf Farm.)

ELMENDORF DINING ROOM. This comfortable, cozy dining room, used for intimate dinner parties, is a part of Elmendorf Farm. (Courtesy of Anne Peters.)

ELMENDORF LIBRARY. This was a place for relaxing and for men to gather after dinner parties to smoke their cigars and drink their brandy. (Courtesy of Anne Peters.)

ELMENDORF DRAWING ROOM. After dinner, while the men frequently gathered in the library, the women would join together in the drawing room. (Courtesy of Anne Peters.)

ENTRANCE IN ITS HEYDAY. Today at Elmendorf, there are lovely trees and shrubs filling in at this entrance. (Courtesy of Anne Peters.)

AT GAINSBOROUGH FARM. A proud mother shows off her new baby at Gainsborough Farm. She is keeping an eye on the photographer and will, if necessary, put herself between baby and man. (Courtesy of author; photograph by John Archambeault.)

STALLION BARN, BLUEGRASS COUNTRY. This is a photograph of a stallion barn in Central Kentucky. This building is where stallions live their days and have their own personal paddock area. (Courtesy of author; photograph by James Archambeault.)

MIDDLEBROOK FARM. Texas longhorns lounge on Middlebrook Farm in the midst of mares and foals. (Courtesy of author.)

OVERBROOK FARM, LEXINGTON, KENTUCKY. Overbrook Farm, located on Delong Road, was founded by William T. Young in 1972. It is easy to tell from the entrance to the farm that Young liked his privacy. Rather than live on the farm, Young preferred to live in Lexington with his wife, Lucy Hilton Maddox Young, because his son, W. T. Young Jr., and grandchildren were nearby. Two of his most famous horses are Storm Cat and 1996 Kentucky Derby winner Grindstone. In 2009, W. T. Young Jr. announced the farm's intent to become more of a leasing farm and sell most of the stock. His son, Chris, has an interest in the horse industry like his grandfather and has opted to keep Storm Cat and Grindstone. Storm Cat was pensioned in 2008 and will live out his years at Overbrook. Grindstone currently lives on another farm to finish his breeding seasons but will return to Overbrook when pensioned. (Courtesy of author.)

SPINDLETOP ESTATE, LEXINGTON, KENTUCKY. This is the backyard of Spindletop Estate, currently a private club for University of Kentucky employees and retirees. Today many weddings are performed on the porch under the columns. (Courtesy of author.)

SPENDTHRIFT FARM, LEXINGTON, KENTUCKY. Established in 1937, Spendthrift has been a noted breeding operation for years. Located on Ironworks Pike, home to two Triple Crown winners and nine Kentucky Derby winners, the farm was founded by Leslie Combs. (Courtesy of author.)

SHADWELL FARM, LEXINGTON, KENTUCKY. Established in 1985, Shadwell Racing is the 1,400-acre thoroughbred horse racing operation of the deputy ruler of Dubai, Sheikh Hamdan bin Rashid Al Maktoum. Introduced to thoroughbred flat racing while a student in the United Kingdom, Sheikh Hamdan established his first racing stable there in 1981. Over the years, he has invested heavily in both racing and breeding and has acquired major operations in England, Ireland, and the United States. He owns eight stud farms worldwide. Aljabr, Daaher, Dayjur, Dumaani, Intidab, Invasor, Jazil, Mustanfar, and Swain all currently stand at the farms' stallion division, Nashwan Stud. Shadwell's most famous broodmare is Height of Fashion, who was sold by Queen Elizabeth II to Sheikh Hamdan Al Maktoum after setting a new course record in the Princess of Wales's Stakes. (Courtesy of author.)

WALNUT HALL FARM, LEXINGTON, KENTUCKY. Walnut Hall, located on Newtown Pike, was originally part of a land grant by Patrick Henry to William Christian as a reward for his service in the Revolutionary War. Lamon Harkness purchased 400 acres of this land and established the Walnut Hill Stock Farm. This standardbred operation is one of the oldest farms in the United States and is still operated by the same family. (Courtesy of author.)

WINSTAR FARM, VERSAILLES, KENTUCKY. WinStar, located on Pisgah Pike, is comprised of approximately 1,400 acres, including a portion that was formerly the Silver Pond Farm. WinStar is home to Bluegrass Cat, Tiznow, and many others. The farm is co-owned by Kenny Troutt and chairman Bill Casner. The two business partners formed Excel Communications. Successful in that endeavor, which later went public, the two opted to form another successful partnership, establishing WinStar Farm. WinStar is clearly one of the more beautiful farms in Central Kentucky. Each farm entrance is named in honor of their horses. WinStar is famous for breeding Kentucky Derby champion Funny Cide. (Courtesy of author.)

FAIRYDOM. Fairydom is pictured at the Keeneland Racecourse in Lexington, Kentucky, in October 1970. She raced in allowance and claiming races. Fairydom died while foaling. Gene Thompson is pictured on the far left. (Courtesy of Gene Thompson.)

HORSES GRAZING OFF OLD FRANKFORT PIKE. These horses are waiting for the sun to rise. In summer, horses are put out at night to protect their coats from bleaching out, particularly if they are going to the sales. (Courtesy of C. Morgan-Cornett.)

STALLION BARN. These horses are grazing in a pasture outside of a stallion barn on an early summer day in Lexington. (Courtesy of author; photograph by Jeff Durham.)

FOALS ENJOYING THEIR BACKYARD. Two young foals are enjoying a cool morning. The young foals will go out with the mothers and play and graze at night to protect their coats. During the day they will return to their stalls, where their mother will be fed and watered. Fans are used to make them comfortable during the day. (Courtesy of C. Morgan-Cornett.)

HORSES GRAZING. These horses are grazing at Three Chimneys Farm. Racehorses love being turned out to graze. Because they are athletes, they do not like being penned up too long. (Courtesy of C. Morgan-Cornett.)

PRACTICE RACING. A horse practices running at Never More Stables. Thoroughbreds are born and bred to run, and when out in paddocks, they take off running the perimeters. (Courtesy of C. Morgan-Cornett.)

MARE AND HER FOAL PLAYING. A mare and her foal are shown playing together. Young foals learn to jump, run, and play at an early age. They also keep close to their mother's side. (Courtesy of C. Morgan-Cornett.)

GRAVE SITE OF ALYDAR. Most horse farms have their own cemeteries for their racehorses. The graves are well taken care of and have very nice head stones. Alydar will now be remembered and visited for years to come. (Courtesy of author.)

112

FOAL PLAYING. A foal plays on Three Chimneys Farm. It is recess time, and like kids, the foals get together and play hard. Their mothers probably hope they will wear themselves out. (Courtesy of C. Morgan-Cornett.)

WHO ARE YOU LOOKING AT? A mare and her foal investigate the photographer. Curiosity is in the nature of some horses. A relatively new mother is going to keep her distance and be prepared to protect her foal. (Courtesy of C. Morgan-Cornett.)

WHO CAN JUMP HIGHER? A mare and her foal are shown here either exercising or playing. This is a fun time for all parents, and horses are no exception. Horses are sociable creatures and relate well with each other. (Courtesy of C. Morgan-Cornett.)

MOM AND ME. A foal plays while its mother stays close by. It is their version of a backyard, and while mom is busy with other things, she is still alert and aware of what her youngster is doing. (Courtesy of C. Morgan-Cornett.)

GATHERING TO PLAN THE MORNING ACTIVITY. A frosty morning in Kentucky energizes these horses. Anyone for a game of soccer? (Courtesy of C. Morgan-Cornett.)

IS THIS THE TEASER? This unusually marked horse is not a racehorse, but he lives with them and teases them without getting into trouble. (Courtesy of C. Morgan-Cornett.)

A Picture to Wake Up to. This peaceful scene is someone's backyard, and this is what they wake up to every morning. (Courtesy of author.)

I Won the Derby. Smarty Jones looks to see who is looking at him. (Courtesy of C. Morgan-Cornett.)

YOU WANT TO TAKE A PICTURE OF ME? Big Brown, pictured at Three Chimneys Farm, occupies himself with watching what is going on in his barn. (Courtesy of C. Morgan-Cornett.)

THAT SUN SURE FEELS GOOD. This mother and foal are taking their afternoon nap on this mid-afternoon winter day. (Courtesy of C. Morgan-Cornett.)

I Have to Work? These horses are in training at Never More Stables. The early part of training is getting horses used to being handled by people and then comfortable with tack. These horses are in the early phases. (Courtesy of C. Morgan-Cornett.)

Bluegrass Area Ice Storm. A 2009 ice storm on Iron Works Pike was hard on horses, as the water in the paddocks froze and the ground was cold and slippery. Farm employees took care of the horses, breaking the ice over the water for them. If the ground became too slippery, the employees would bring the horses into the barn. (Courtesy of C. Morgan-Cornett.)

I Said I Do Not Want My Picture Taken. This foal is on Middlebrook Farm. (Courtesy of C. Morgan-Cornett.)

NAP TIME FOR THE CHILDREN. Twin foals are a rarity in thoroughbred horses, and like any mother, this mare is getting her lunch as quickly as she can before tending to the children, again. (Courtesy of C. Morgan-Cornett.)

THE FINISH LINE IS JUST AROUND THE CORNER. There are two important places jockeys look for while horse racing: the quarter pole, when the jockey will relax his hold on 1200 pounds of horse to take off full steam, and the finish line. These competitors are racing at Keeneland Race Course in Lexington, KY. (Courtesy of Karen Pulliam; photograph by James Archambeault.)

HORSE FARM CEMETERIES. Horse farms have their own cemeteries. Most horses have only their head, heart, and four hooves buried when they die, but an extremely remarkable horse will frequently be buried whole, such as Secretariat and Man O' War. (Both courtesy of author.)

ALMOST THERE. Horses are racing to the finish line on a Kentucky track. (Courtesy of author; photograph by Dan Dry.)

THE CALM BEFORE THE STORM. This photograph of the modern Churchill Downs was taken during the off-season, one month before the fall meet in 2009. It is very quiet compared to derby day. (Courtesy of author.)

ANOTHER WIN FOR WILLIE.
Ferdinand's rider, Willie Shoemaker
(left), talks to the outrider
after winning the Kentucky
Derby. (Courtesy of author.)

FOCUSED ON THEIR BUSINESS. Jockeys
are going to the paddock to meet
with the horses they will be riding
in the race. (Courtesy of author.)

My Old Kentucky Home
Words and Music by: Stephen C. Foster

The sun shines bright in the old Kentucky home
'Tis summer, the people are gay;
The corn top's ripe and the meadow's in the bloom,
While the birds make music all the day;
The young folks roll on the little cabin floor,
All merry, all happy, and bright,
By'n by hard times comes a-knocking at the door,
Then my old Kentucky home, good night!

Chorus

Weep no more, my lady,
Oh weep no more today!
We will sing one song for the old Kentucky home,
For the old Kentucky home far away.

They hunt no more for the 'possum and the coon,
On meadow, the hill and the shore,
They sing no more by the glimmer of the moon,
On the bench by the old cabin door;
The day goes by like a shadow o'er the heart,
With sorrow where all was delight;
The time has come when the people have to part,
Then my old Kentucky home, good night!

Chorus

The head must bow and the back will have to bend,
Wherever the people may go;
A few more days and the trouble all will end
In the field where sugar-canes may grow;
A few more days for to tote the weary load,
No matter, 'twill never be light,
A few more days till we totter on the road,
Then my old Kentucky home, good night!

MY OLD KENTUCKY HOME. The most famous song on Kentucky Derby day is "My Old Kentucky Home" by Stephen Foster. These words can be easily remembered, and the chorus is a tearjerker for Kentuckians who are away from their home state on derby day. (Courtesy of author.)

GLOSSARY

Note: In thoroughbred horse racing, there is no artificial insemination, and all thoroughbred horses share the birthday of January 1, regardless of their actual birth date.

breaks maiden—first race the horse wins
breeding—the act of horses mating or the horse's bloodline
broodmare—adult female horses who are breeding
colt—male horses under four years old
cover—the mare is covered by the stallion in the breeding process
dam or "out of"—mother of horse
farrier—blacksmith
fillie—female horse under four years old
foal—baby horse
foaled— a mare has given birth
gelding—castrated male horse
in foal—mare is pregnant
maiden—has never won a race
mare—adult female horse
mudder—racehorse performs well on muddy track
pensioned—completely retired, no racing or breeding allowed
retired—retired from racing and breeding
stallion—male horse that has not been castrated
stud—male horses ready for breeding
slipped—mare has miscarried her foal
sired, or "by"—father of horse
stakes race—race conditions met before being allowed to enter and are graded I, II, or III
stud fee—fee paid to the stallion owner(s) for a successful breeding
stands and nurses—indicates stud fee is paid when newborn foal stands up and nurses
up—jockey riding the horse

BIBLIOGRAPHY

Denbo, Bruce and Mary Wharton. *The Horse World of the Bluegrass*. Portland, ME: John Bradford, 1980.

Garrison, Richard, Sydney S. Combs, and J. Winston Coleman. *Old Homes of the Bluegrass*. Lexington, KY: The Kentucky Society, 1950.

Wright, John D. *Lexington Heart of the Bluegrass*. Lexington, KY: Lexington Fayette County History Com, 1982.

Kerr, Bettie L. and John D. Wright Jr. *Lexington: A Century in Photographs*. Lexington, KY: Lexington Fayette County History Com, 1984.

For more information about various horse farms, visit www.directoryoftheturf.com.

www.arcadiapublishing.com

MAP SEARCH

Discover books about the town where you grew up, the cities where your friends and families live, the town where your parents met, or even that retirement spot you've been dreaming about. Our Web site provides history lovers with exclusive deals, advanced notification about new titles, e-mail alerts of author events, and much more.

MADE IN THE USA

Arcadia Publishing, the leading local history publisher in the United States, is committed to making history accessible and meaningful through publishing books that celebrate and preserve the heritage of America's people and places. Consistent with our mission to preserve history on a local level, this book was printed in South Carolina on American-made paper and manufactured entirely in the United States.

This book carries the accredited Forest Stewardship Council (FSC) label and is printed on 100 percent FSC-certified paper. Products carrying the FSC label are independently certified to assure consumers that they come from forests that are managed to meet the social, economic, and ecological needs of present and future generations.

FSC
Mixed Sources
Product group from well-managed forests and other controlled sources

Cert no. SW-COC-001530
www.fsc.org
© 1996 Forest Stewardship Council

Find Your Place in History.